AUFTRAGSTAKTIK
The Birth of Enlightened Leadership

PRAISE FOR AUFTRAGSTAKTIK

The courage to analytically face the leadership principles of other nations and to reflect on them is admirable. Colonel Oliviero has succeeded masterfully. After all, what else is there? Tactics, mastering the principles of combat, always remain piecemeal if the leader hasn't also mastered the essential principles of leadership. Tactical building blocks need the mortar of leadership to form a solid wall on the battlefield. But where those tactical building blocks leave gaps, the well-led subordinate must know what the goal is. He must act and take initiative according to the given order, even if the superior is not available at the moment. This Führen mit Auftrag can only be learned to a limited extent. The combat leader must feel it and so too must the subordinates. Only thus can troops be successful, even outnumbered. A book well worth reading.
- **Karl Ernst Graf von Strachwitz General der Aufklärungstruppe**

Col Oliviero has written a succinct and very readable account of the development of Auftragstaktik as a leadership philosophy which, at its best inspired the outstanding battlefield performance of the Prussian and German Armies. He rightly praises the strongest elements of the Prussian-German military tradition - the creation of a dedicated General Staff, the sustained study and practise of operational art, the acceptance of chaos as the fundamental nature of war - but also acknowledges the weaknesses which resulted from the tradition of direct loyalty to the head of state, whether Hohenzollern monarch or Hitler.

He concludes by pointing out that the adoption of Mission Command as a command philosophy in other armies, while persisting in micromanagement, excessive focus on technology, and intolerance of failure, is unlikely to lead to similar success!
- **Lieutenant General Sir William Raoul Rollo, KCB, CBE former Deputy of UK Defence Staff**

Peter Drucker famously said that culture eats strategy for breakfast. While this quote primarily refers to the concept of business and organizational culture, it is very much pertinent to the context presented by Colonel (retired) Oliviero in his new book Auftragstaktik. The attempts by the Canadian Army and many of its allies to adopt and inculcate the critical and proven concepts of German Mission Command and Manoeuvre Warfare into their doctrine – an inadequate Anglo-Saxon translation of the term Auftragstaktik - have floundered. Chuck's in-depth understanding of this German environment, gained through detailed study and personal experience, enables the reader to gain a clear understanding of those factors.

Just as he did in his book Strategia, Chuck provides an enlightened insight on this critical topic and will elicit a profound reflection that will guide the professional development of those interested in military history, culture, and leadership philosophy.
- **Lieutenant-General JM Lanthier, MSM, CD, former Vice Chief of the Canadian Armed Forces Defence Staff**

Enlightened Leadership is a comprehensive and thoughtful explanation of the rise of the Prussian Way of War that is the foundation of our modern doctrines of Mission Command and Manoeuvre warfare. Chuck Oliviero makes a compelling case however that without an understanding of the cultural, social, and historical bases of the Prusso-German school's Auftragstaktik it is impossible to achieve Mission Command in the way that NATO doctrine writers have envisaged. In paying lip service to these profound concepts without a contextual understanding of their evolution we risk professional failure. We would do well to incorporate this message into our body of professional knowledge and practice.

**- Major General Michael J. Ward, MSC, CD, former Commander
of the Canadian Army Doctrine and Training Command**

"You can't grow cactus in the tundra." This simple quotation from one of his professors at RMC sums up Col Oliviero's book about Auftragstaktik. For too long, Anglo-Saxon militaries have tried to implement "Mission Tactics" or "Maneuver Warfare" as our English-speaking version of German Operational Doctrine. Or, more rightly, as Col Oliviero argues, an entire Prusso-German military culture of which Mission Orders are only a small part. We are uprooting the cactus and trying to grow it in the tundra. To do this successfully, we need to terraform the tundra. Chuck's book is the first step in understanding that wise leaders in the American, British, Canadian, and Australian forces should begin to terra-form our tundra to grow that German cactus. But as he rightly points out, we must leave the rattlesnakes of racism and the gila monsters of militarism back in that old German desert.

- Dr. John "Doc" Broom, PhD, AFRHistS Norwich University.

Chuck writes passionately about key leadership issues: mission, shared responsibility, and trust. He exposes the inherit flaws in modern mission command doctrine which misinterprets Auftragstaktik. Through his deep knowledge of Prussian military history, Chuck provides all commanders with fresh insights into the cultural, organizational, and political roots of this battle-winning concept.

**Colonel Eric MacArthur, CD former
Chief of Staff Canadian Forces College**

Chuck's deep dive in the historical German record is a stimulating account not only of the historical underpinnings of the concept itself but also of the evolution of his personal intellectual journey to understand how it evolved from German historical traditions and cultural practices. He raises fundamental questions about the fusion of military and social cultures. This book should be a must-read for military professionals of any army, and anyone interested in military history, war, and society. Read on.

**- Dr. Bill McAndrew, PhD, former historian at the Canadian
Directorate of History**

AUFTRAGSTAKTIK

The Birth of Enlightened Leadership

by

Colonel Charles S. Oliviero

DOUBLE‡DAGGER
— www.doubledagger.ca —

Library and Archives Canada Cataloguing in Publication
Oliviero, Charles S. author
Auftragstaktik / Charles S. Oliviero

Issued in print and electronic formats.
ISBN: 978-1-990644-37-5 (soft cover)
ISBN: 978-1-990644-38-2 (e-book)

Editor: Eric MacArthur / Phil Halton
Cover design: Pablo Javier Herrera
Interior Design: Winston A. Prescott

Cover: The image is a detail from Georg Bleibtreu's painting of the Battle of Königgrätz, 1866.

Double Dagger Books Ltd
Toronto, Ontario, Canada
www.doubledagger.ca

DEDICATION

Ich schwöre, der Bundesrepublik Deutschland treu zu dienen, und das Recht und die Freiheit des deutschen Volkes tapfer zu verteidigen, so wahr mir Gott helfe.

I swear to loyally serve the Federal Republic of Germany and to courageously defend the rights and the liberty of the German people, so help me God.

I dedicate this volume to my brother officers from the 29th course (1986-1988) of Germany's Command and General Staff College in Hamburg. *Die Führungsakademie der Bundeswehr.*

My *Klassenkameraden*, through their patience, assistance and most importantly, their friendship, during my two years at the world's oldest military school provided me with not only the best possible professional military education but also with an opening to a philosophy of leadership, enlightened leadership, that I had read about but never seen in practice.

As discussed in the *Epilogue*, these men were the heirs of a proud military tradition. The incident described in that section was but a single example of how seriously these officers took their professional responsibilities and I am proud to have been among them.

Lastly, I offer a special thought for one of our NATO

classmates and brother Hussar, who did not live to graduate with us. Major Hans Berkhout, i.G., Royal Dutch Hussars, tragically passed away before course end. I'll see you on the objective, my friend.

ABSTRACT

To greater or lesser degrees, all thirty NATO members espouse the doctrine of Manoeuvre Warfare as the preferred method of fighting. One of the pillars of this modern doctrine is the concept of Mission Command, which is the English translation of what the Germans call *Auftragstaktik*. Although widely practised and discussed in military circles, *Auftragstaktik* remains poorly understood. Outside of Germany, *Auftragstaktik* is seen most often as an outgrowth of German *Blitzkrieg* tactics from the Second World War. But the leadership philosophy of *Auftragstaktik* traces its genesis to a time before Germany existed. *Auftragstaktik* truly began to flower during the Napoleonic Wars, the creation of the world's first professional military, and to the subsequent reforms of the Prussian army after 1806. In conjunction with the development of the General Staff system, the Prussian army created two unique warfighting tools, which when combined created a unique Prusso-German School of War.

Much has been written regarding the first of these innovations, the Great General Staff, but the other tool, *Auftragstaktik*, the second integral element of this unique understanding of war, remains clouded in misinterpretation. More than just a tool, this leadership philosophy, triggered by a devastating battlefield defeat, was expanded, and refined throughout the 19th century. During its development, it became the foundation of Prussian success in three European wars. Later, it became the key to German tactical excellence.

For modern NATO forces to properly integrate *Auftragstaktik* into their collective doctrines requires a better understanding of its origins and development. This book affords that understanding. This volume uncovers the early intellectual and structural changes undergone by the Prussian army, from before the French Revolution to the eve of the First World War, with a glimpse at the interwar period. It thereby provides the necessary background and understanding, without which *Auftragstaktik* cannot become part of a shared interoperable military doctrine among NATO partners – if at all.

TABLE OF CONTENTS

FOREWORD

T oo soon old, too late smart. I am pushing ninety years now and wish that I had had the opportunity to read Chuck Oliviero's history of the development of *Auftragstaktik* many years ago when I was trying to understand the differences between the German and Canadian/British ways of war, their tactical doctrines. They seemed to be based on quite different premises and exercised command differently. The German system seemed so flexible. For instance, it was remarkable how the Germans were able to recover from the surprise Allied landing at Anzio and stop the advance towards Rome when they had no major units in the vicinity. Their supreme commander appointed a task force commander and gave him the simple mission to stop the advance. He, in turn, gathered up a disparate force of retreating soldiers, cooks, drivers, and whoever else was in the area, deployed them as small groups, and gave them the same simple mission – deny the advance in their immediate area. The mission remained the same on down the line. It worked, but how? Another example intrigued me: why a regimental commander was denied a very senior decoration for leading his regiment personally in a hand-to-hand assault. The report said that the physical courage he displayed was expected behaviour of a regimental commander; the award would only be given to a commander who took at least two independent operational decisions. Yet another instance was when a Sergeant-Major was not disciplined for refusing to blow up the Roman bridge in Rimini as he had been ordered to do. It was because he had made an independent decision not to blow it because the Allies had by-passed the bridge making it tactically irrelevant. Devolution of responsibility seems to have been imbedded in the system.

What was it in German army operational practice that not just encouraged independent decision making but based its military doctrine on it? It seemed to be unique. So, I was delighted when Chuck told me that he was writing a book on *Auftragstaktik*. My first reaction was that there could be no one better qualified to write it. As a regimental tank commander in the Canadian Army, fluent in English, French, Italian and German, he had survived the rigorous regime of the German Army Command and General Staff College and after retiring, completed his doctorate in war studies. This deep practical and theoretical background has given Chuck a superlative grounding in comparative military affairs.

I met Chuck when he was on the Directing Staff at the Canadian Army Command and Staff College and arranged battlefield studies of Canadian operations in Italy and Normandy during the Second World War. I conducted the studies on the ground, providing historical context along with Canadian and German veterans of the operations who accompanied us. It was there that I became aware of the range of his military knowledge especially listening to his conversations with the German veterans. At the time I was exploring possible connections between soldiers' behaviour in battle with their tactical doctrine and the concept of *Auftragstaktik* offered an intriguing explanation of connections. One German veteran remarked that the concept made his soldiers shareholders of operations; Canadian soldiers were more or less considered to be 'un-consulted employees', a distinct cultural difference.

My understanding of the concept was superficial, lacking knowledge of its breadth and depth. Chuck's book provides both and much more. His deep dive in the historical German record is a stimulating account not only of the historical underpinnings of the concept itself but also of the evolution of his personal intellectual journey to understand how it evolved from German historical traditions and cultural practices. He raises fundamental questions about the fusion of military and social cultures and considers if those unique German practices can easily be applied in cultures with their own different norms.

This book should be a must read for military professionals of any army, and anyone interested in military history, war, and society. Read on.

Professor William McAndrew, PhD
Ottawa, Ontario
2022

PREFACE

I n 1986, I was a young major in the Royal Canadian Armoured Corps. During my professional military education studies as a captain at the Canadian Army Command and Staff College, I became intrigued by the battlefield successes of various German armies through the centuries. This interest led me to *Auftragstaktik*, a word which was as alien to me in its precepts as it was in its pronunciation. I began to read more widely about this leadership philosophy, but information was scarce and most literature, being in American military publications such as *Military Review*, *Parameters*, or the *US Marine Corps Gazette*, was filtered through American understandings of battlefield leadership and how the German concept might help American military leaders during its post-Vietnam revitalization.

Just over a year after being introduced to this philosophy, I was coincidently selected to attend the two-year Command and General Staff Course of the German Armed Forces Command and General Staff College, located in the *Clausewitz Kaserne* in Hamburg, West Germany. The *Führungsakademie der Bundeswehr* (FüAk) was the modern incarnation of Prussia's famous *Kriegsakademie*. After a year of intensive language study in the Canadian Forces Language School in Ottawa, I packed up my small family and headed for Hamburg. Having only ever visited Germany twice before, and only for a couple of weeks, the looming experience was both exciting and daunting.

Once settled and launched on the course, I quickly came to realize that much more so than at the Canadian Army Command and Staff College, the FüAk course was deeply steeped in tactics, operations, and the requisite staff work. Each day brought new techniques, new ideas and nuances to battlefield leadership that had heretofore been unknown to me, or like *Auftragstaktik*, misunderstood due to faulty translations. Working almost exclusively in German brought a broader spectrum of understanding of German battlefield leadership than I had attained through my mostly American – and British-influenced study.

I had always been blessed with an innate language ability (German was my fourth language) and, as I became more fluent, I took the opportunity to engage more widely with fellow students, instructors, and senior German officers on the historical basis, first for *Blitzkrieg* (it was a media myth) and then later, and more importantly, for *Auftragstaktik*. The FüAk library was a veritable treasure trove of memoirs, manuals, and military history and I immersed myself in the German texts. The more I read, the more I realized just how multifaceted the philosophy underlying *Auftragstaktik* was. This was no simple leadership tool.

Concurrent with my attendance at the FüAk, NATO armies, led almost in tandem (but in competition) by the US Army and the British Army, were also discovering *Auftragstaktik* and looking at the possibility of incorporating this concept into their respective leadership doctrines. Exactly how this came about is an interesting story on its own and it is deeply intertwined with the introduction of a new doctrine with the unfortunate nomenclature of Maneuver Warfare. More on that later. Simultaneously, the two great Anglo-Saxon allies had embraced Operational Art (*Operative Kunst*), a level of war that the Germans had long claimed as their own. *Operative Kunst* necessitated the type of freedom of action (*Freiheit des Handelns*) that *Auftragstaktik* demanded – and to some extent – guaranteed.

One day during my studies in Hamburg, I chanced upon the

British Army Liaison Officer to the FüAk. I mentioned my interest in *Auftragstaktik* and he shared with me a document that he asked me to keep secret. I have done so but, considering the time that has elapsed, I am certain that he would not mind me sharing the contents now. The document was a military letter sent from his German counterpart at the British Army Staff College, Camberley. The German reported back to his superiors that the young British students were clamoring to know more about two deeply German concepts that the German students and he, the exchange officer, constantly mentioned: *Auftragstaktik* and *Operative Kunst*. The report went on to say that the British Directing Staff was not at all happy about this introduction of German tactical doctrine into the Camberley classrooms and that the instructors were doing their best to quash this interest. I was stunned. I wondered aloud why the British Directing Staff was so averse to new concepts. The Liaison Officer just smiled and shrugged.

One of our course prerequisites was to write a long essay on a military topic, the so-called *Jahresarbeit*. I wrote mine on the new concept of Maneuver Warfare, as introduced by William S. Lind, an American civilian who was fascinated by military affairs. Originally introduced in a 1980 article for the *Marine Corps Gazette*, his article "Defining Maneuver Warfare for the Marine Corps" offered the reader a new philosophy of warfare. Later, he published The Maneuver Warfare Handbook, which I found in the FüAk library. My research for that paper answered the question of why the British staff college was resisting German concepts. The British Army of the day remained wedded to strong positional defence tactics and to the battlefield notion that it was a commander's duty to impose order during the battle: two concepts that were anathema to German *Kriegskunst*. My essay was later published in the official journal of the Canadian Armed Forces, the first article written by a Canadian about Maneuver Warfare. Interestingly, all the feedback I received from Canadian army officers was negative. Some of my old friends who were naval officers instantly related to my argument since what I was describing was war at sea!

After graduation, I was fortunate to return to regimental

duty and when I took command of a tank squadron and later of a tank regiment, I did my best to apply what I had learned from my German studies. Interestingly, during the intervening time, Canada and NATO embraced both Maneuver Warfare and a concept called Mission Command (a bad translation of *Auftragstaktik*). The earlier critique of my article was forgotten as the Canadian Army fully (and badly) embraced Maneuver Warfare.

When I joined the staff of the 1st Canadian Division Headquarters in Kingston, Ontario, I began my long quest to gain a PhD. I was then in my forties and my research skills were sadly lacking. I had the good fortune of having Professor Brian McKercher as my first professor in the Royal Military College of Canada MA program. His demanding teaching methods forced me to learn what I did not know and that, combined with RMC's excellent library, which includes a vast collection of German military texts (The Crerar Collection), relaunched my interest in *Auftragstaktik* – but now with a modicum of research skills.

There was a great deal more information about this German leadership philosophy but still almost exclusively in American (and occasionally British) military journals. Eventually, in 1993, Dirk W. Oetting wrote the only historical investigation specifically on the subject, but only in German. I decided to write my MA dissertation on the subject and with Dr McKercher's agreement to act as my thesis supervisor, I began my project. Most of what follows is based on a combination of my German experience and that academic dissertation, edited for ease of reading.

Last, I would like to say a few words about the socio-political beliefs of Prusso-German military. The Prusso-German military of the 17th, 18th, and 19th centuries was uniquely pro-monarchist, anti-democratic, and arguably racist. Many excellent studies on Prussian militarism and their reactionary politics can easily be found and I can recommend them to you. But this is a side issue here and I have avoided as much as possible trying to describe the complex inner workings of the Prusso-German political construct as well as commenting on the social beliefs of the German officer corps, grounded as it was upon ancient Prussian *Junker* tradition. This Prussian tradition and its consequent *Weltanschauung* became the basis of many of the negative aspects of militarism, which led Germany to ruin and ultimate collapse pursuant to the two world wars of the 20th century. This militarism and all its negative trappings are independent of the central theme of the present study, which is focused primarily upon the unique philosophy of leadership, of *Auftragstaktik*, which sprang from the Prussian military.

Nothing in my study should be understood in any way to support the many negative aspects that resided in the Prussian military tradition. Naturally, no philosophic concept stands alone but, in so far as it is possible, I have attempted to highlight the positive aspects of this leadership methodology, while leaving behind the undesirable traditions whence it may have sprung.

By design, I have limited the scope of this work but there are some aspects of *Auftragstaktik* which demonstrate its inextricable connection to the manifold other characteristics of the Prusso-German military tradition. Though strictly speaking, my examples fall outside the period in question and highlight situations that may not be directly related to how this concept was formed, I felt it important to include them in this study and have done so in a series of independent annexes.

Colonel (Retd) Charles S. Oliviero, CD, PhD
Victoria, British Columbia
2022

Frederick II (the Great) of Prussia
Oil painting by Anton Graf, 1781

INTRODUCTION

Le monde ne repose pas plus sûrement sur les épaules d'Atlas que la Prusse sur une telle armée.

- Frederick II of Prussia

uch of the current wisdom within military circles attributes the astounding battlefield successes achieved by German military forces during the last century to the almost mythical leadership concept of *Auftragstaktik*. This uniquely German philosophy has been translated by the United States Army, and subsequently by NATO, into *Mission Command*. This uniquely German term defies such superficial translation. This concept is much more than just a battle-winning technique. It is a highly complex leadership philosophy that encompasses the entire history and spectrum of German socio-military culture. Based upon an historical development deeply rooted in the German Enlightenment (*die Aufklärung*) and forged in the fires of the Napoleonic Wars and the German Wars of Unification, this philosophy is not a product that can be lifted from a shelf and employed. As tempting as it might be, *Auftragstaktik* is anything but rote battlefield technique that can be readily and selectively employed by any military at will.

Auftragstaktik, linked by history and culture to German fighting forces, does not stand alone as a leadership attitude, methodology or philosophy. Although it is all these things, it does not exist in isolation. It never has. This philosophy, demanding mutual trust and respect, is deeply rooted in the blood-soaked soil of German battlefields. Despite this fact, in the attempt to grasp *Auftragstaktik* and employ it, foreign users have too often treated it as a separate, or self-contained, tool. The major English-speaking NATO staff colleges now teach the doctrine of Mission Command or *Auftragstaktik* as if it were a simple technique, which one can choose to draw upon (or not) in any given circumstance. This interpretation is flawed; the concept is foreign to the Anglo-Saxon warfighting tradition and came to NATO through contact with the modern *Bundeswehr*.[1] Thus, an incomplete understanding of its roots is shared, and often even unwittingly fostered, among the American, British, and Canadian armed forces.

In truth, *Auftragstaktik* is only one component of a highly complex and interconnected command and control culture. The translation of *Auftragstaktik* into English as Mission Command demonstrates a fundamental misinterpretation of its meaning; it demonstrates H.L. Mencken's common error of seeking a simple solution to a complex problem, famously writing in 1917 that there was always a well-known and simple solution to every problem – neat, plausible, and wrong! Despite this misunderstanding, Mission Command has been incorporated into British, American, and Canadian military doctrine as a style of leadership; this style inexplicably being expected to stand on its own. Yet, the idea has been taken from the modern *Bundeswehr* with little or no appreciation of the historical background or the cultural baggage, which accompanies the term. This 'conceptual grafting' of one doctrine upon another denies the very nature of *Auftragstaktik* by separating it from its history.

Considering this fundamental error, it would be naive to believe that what worked for the Germans will automatically work for other armed forces serving other political cultures and societies. Of course, foreign concepts can be imported into any native culture but doing so is neither a straightforward nor a simple process. Conceptual grafting must be done with great care, both for the concept being brought in and for the new host. As my old friend and mentor, Professor Bill McAndrew used to like to say, 'You can't grow cactus in the tundra.'

Transferring a cultural norm from one society to another was no small task. It was far more difficult than simply borrowing a belief system of a procedure and dropping it into the lap of the new host culture. No one has seriously suggested that NATO should adopt the thousand-year-old Japanese philosophy of *Bushido* as a leadership technique. Such a suggestion surely seems risible. This is not because Bushido is not an effective leadership method; it is. This philosophy underlying the ancient cult of the Japanese *Samurai* has proven capable of motivating soldiers to perform almost superhuman feats of bravery and selflessness. The reason that *Bushido* has not been introduced into NATO is simple enough: the obvious cultural and historical roots of the Japanese warrior culture are completely foreign to Europeans and North Americans. Grafting this philosophy would be extremely difficult. Yet, the cultural issue of introducing *Auftragstaktik* has not been seen as an obstacle.

After the end of the Second World War, there began in military circles a great and abiding fascination with the *Wehrmacht*[2] and its tactical doctrine. Later, Colonel Trevor N. Dupuy, US Army (Ret), wrote extensively on the perceived combat superiority of the German Army. He was by no means the only one. By the mid-1980s, most English-speaking professional military journals had published articles extolling the efficacy of the German military machine and used this proficiency to explain how a country that was so numerically inferior had conquered nearly all of Europe and then held out against the Allies for as long as it did. Thus, among many NATO armies, the tactical doctrine of the *Wehrmacht* became a *cause célèbre*.

Over time, with the increasing power and concomitant integration of Germany and the *Bundeswehr* into NATO affairs, more and more military officers were exposed to German tactical doctrine. The growing shared military experience among the three major allied partners, America, Great Britain, and then Germany – after it began to rebuild its armed forces in 1956 – became a major feature of the alliance, especially after the withdrawal of the French military from the allied structure. By the early 1980s, many British and American officers had come to the realization that, despite their defeat, there was much of value in German military doctrine. About this time in the United States, William Lind, a civilian but someone who was fascinated by military affairs, coined the term "Maneuver Warfare" in an article in the *Marine Corps Gazette*. His article, "Defining Maneuver Warfare for the Marine Corps" proposed a new philosophy of warfare. The historical basis for Lind's thesis was based partly upon the ancient writings of Sun Tzu, which also drew

3

extensively upon the *Wehrmacht* experience in the Second World War and so, not surprisingly, one of the key tools of this new philosophy of warfare was *Auftragstaktik*. Lind's research may have been shallow, but the article gripped the imagination of a generation of military leaders and thereby launched a renaissance in military thinking. Studying the battlefield successes of the German army during the Second World War soon gained the significance and legitimacy that formerly it had lacked. Consequently, the study went from being a hobby to being a legitimate part of professional military education.

During the 1980s and 1990s, perhaps no single subject generated as much interest and debate as the concept of *Auftragstaktik*. More than any other single idea within what was being heralded as a Revolution in Military Affairs (RMA), *Auftragstaktik* stirred the imaginations of amateurs and professionals alike. It became the subject of articles in such diverse military journals as the US Naval Institute *Proceedings*, the US Army Command and Staff College *Military Review*, the *Canadian Defence Quarterly*, and the *British Army Review*. *Auftragstaktik* was simultaneously touted as the ultimate battlefield force multiplier as well as denigrated as an unworkable fiction. It was espoused by many as a panacea to solve all tactical problems; it was scorned as a military myth. Unfortunately, although *Auftragstaktik* was for many years a hotly debated topic, due to a dearth of academic material in any language, few managed to come to any more than a passing understanding of what the term means. Eventually, in 1993, Dirk W. Oetting authored the only historical investigation written specifically on the subject. His book, *Auftragstaktik: Geschichte und Gegenwart einer Führungskonzeption*, (*Auftragstaktik*: *History and Presence of a Leadership Concept*) focused on the 20th century, was never translated, and remains obscure.

History is a civilization's collective memory. At an individual level, if one does not know that a dog attacked someone when they were young, they might find it odd that they should be terrified by a Labrador Retriever who comes looking to be petted. So, too, with cultures. Without knowing the origins or preconditions of a given cultural norm or practice, it is difficult if not impossible to fully understand it. Thus, the first step in attempting to gain some deeper understanding of *Auftragstaktik* is to appreciate that this concept was the product neither of modern Germany nor of the Nazi *Reichswehr*. The foundations of *Auftragstaktik* were laid long before the wars of the 20th century. Despite the age of this venerable philosophy, the historical development of *Auftragstaktik* remains an almost unstudied field. Consequently, there is a dearth of information available on the subject.

Although practised by German leaders for generations, only Oetting's book covers the subject in German and there are none in English. Further, Oetting's work focuses on modern practices. It is my intent, therefore, to contribute to a better general understanding of this practice, which although widely used, remains poorly understood, by beginning my investigation before *Auftragstaktik* came into being. In this way, a solid foundation can be established upon which a solid understanding can be built.

First, it is important to appreciate what this work is *not*. It is not an etymological study. It is not a chronological tracking of a tactical term. It is not an attempt to view the development of a tactical tool in isolation. A mere chronological study of events leading to the modern term *Auftragstaktik* does not offer an historical appreciation. Rather, this study is an investigation of the interrelation of the military, political, social, moral, and, most importantly, the intellectual factors that combined and recombined to create a new school of war: the Prusso-German School. This new school of war altered the way that Prussians, and then all Germans, fought their many wars.

This book argues that *Auftragstaktik* was the Prusso-German School's single greatest expression of its uniqueness, and yet even after more than a century, it remains shrouded in myth and mystery. My aim here is to offer a better understanding of this unique leadership philosophy using an investigation into the early development of Prussian and German warfighting as the vehicle for that study. In that vein, this book is an investigation of the evolution of a leadership mechanism as it developed from a single idea into a pivotal and fundamental component of a complete philosophy of how battles are to be planned, fought, and won. My hope is that through gaining a better understanding of how one idea evolved into a complete philosophy, it may indeed be possible to harness *Auftragstaktik* for use outside of the German military.

There are many difficulties facing the student of *Auftragstaktik*, the primary difficulty being one of definition. This challenge does not stem merely from the fact that the word is problematic to translate into English. Even in its native German, the term raises controversy. An etymological search uncovers the fact that the term itself came into usage long after the introduction of the concept. The idea was taught and practised beginning just after the turn of the 19th century, but the term was not commonly used until the 20th. In its most elementary form, *Auftragstaktik* refers to the mutual trust between superiors and subordinates, where superiors set goals, provide resources, and give subordinates free rein to achieve those goals. In its fullest and most elevated applications, it makes all members of a military chain of command mutual participants in the achievement of a mission. There is tacit trust up and down the chain of command and subordinates are allowed even the extreme action of disobedience if it will result in the ultimate achievement of the superior commander's intent. The concept is based upon the pillars of the subordination of self to a superior's goal, upon independent action, and upon freedom of action at all levels. Properly used, *Auftragstaktik* transforms all leaders in a chain of command from being merely involved in a mission to being fully committed to its success.

Because of its complexity, the challenge of gaining a better understanding of how the Prussian army developed *Auftragstaktik* is best accomplished thematically rather than chronologically. Therefore, each of the following chapters takes a major theme and considers it as a separate idea, which when combined with the other major themes, helps to form the bigger picture. The book is therefore divided into thematic chapters. The *Conclusion* brings together all the themes. Last, the *Epilogue* questions whether the modern *Bundeswehr* rightly deserves the moniker of tactical heir to Scharnhorst's Prusso-German School of War. There are also four stand-alone annexes to assist the reader.

Chapter One, *Kriegskunst*, investigates how and why the Prussians, and later the Germans, created their own concepts of warfare. For more than a millennium, the myriad German states fought their wars no differently than did their French, Austrian, Italian, or Swiss neighbours. Then something happened which altered the arc of their military development. Unique in the European experience, Prusso-German military progress thereafter followed a path divergent from all its neighbours.

Chapter Two, *Der Generalstab,* investigates the creation and development of the General Staff system up to the eve of the 20th century. (We stop there because the post-1918 history of the General Staff stands alone). Although staff systems were neither unique nor confined to Germany, the system developed in Prussia and then adopted throughout Greater Germany came to be not only singular, but also the model emulated throughout the world by militaries as different as the US Army and the Japanese Imperial Army.

Chapter Three, *Führen durch Auftrag,* traces the intellectual development that drove tactical change for nearly a century. Beginning with the Napoleonic Wars, Prussian warfare redefined itself while the army simultaneously created a new paradigm for warfare. In order not to confuse the issue with a similar renewal after Versailles in 1918, the full investigation ends before Alfred *Graf* von Schlieffen became the Chief of the Great General Staff in 1891.[34]

Chapter Four, *Auftragstaktik,* brings together the preceding parts. It investigates the Hegelian synthesis that was the product of this near century of battlefield tactical development with the unique staff system begun by the Prussians. Intellectually connecting all these component parts returns us to the NATO Alliance and the attempt among its members to embrace Mission Command.

Chapter Five: *Interregnum,* steps beyond the timespan of the study to briefly look at the post-First World War environment in Germany and the strains that it placed upon the German army and its doctrine.

Chapter Six: *Doctrine,* returns to the thorny issue of the importation of foreign doctrine and how careful any institution must be when attempting to borrow ideas and processes from other, especially foreign, entities.

The *Conclusions* of the study are perhaps controversial. However interesting the question of how to integrate *Auftragstaktik* may be, and what the relation between *Auftragstaktik* and Mission Command is, this matter is cursory to the issue at hand. The reality is that *Auftragstaktik* is so deeply rooted in German culture that the other NATO countries cannot hope to simply adopt this battle-winning philosophy. Despite the best intentions of those who have rewritten the doctrine, it simply cannot be done. The modern pillars of *Auftragstaktik*, even if one discounts the historical and cultural background, can be summarized as trust, training, and simple orders. Neither the current command climate, nor the training philosophy, nor the current philosophy of transmitting orders allows for the prerequisites demanded by *Auftragstaktik*. Without fundamentally rethinking the adoption of this profoundly German command and control philosophy, whether the Alliance can ever hope to integrate *Auftragstaktik* remains moot.

The *Epilogue* investigates whether, after two centuries and so much political and social upheaval, sometimes cataclysmic as was experienced during the twelve-year Nazi regime, the modern rebirth of Germany's military institutions could successfully recapture the excellence of its past without also dragging along some of the questionable moral baggage. To use the words of several German military historians, can Germany and its military ever deal with the trauma of its 'undigested past'?

The four annexes offer related insights but are not, strictly speaking, essential to understanding the history of *Auftragstaktik*'s development. Annexes A and B are offered to assist the reader in keeping straight the many personalities, too often named either Wilhelm or Frederick (or both). Annex C is offered to put into context how the doctrine of *Auftragstaktik* is employed by contemporary soldiers. Last, Annex D looks at how *Auftragstaktik* can move beyond purely military applications to be applied in civilian or corporate environments.

Admittedly or not, the current philosophic underpinnings of the doctrine, which major NATO partners espouse, rely heavily upon the belief that war is more of a science than an art. Whatever the American, British, Canadian, Dutch, and even the French armies may claim, their respective doctrines are *not* Clausewitzian; they are most assuredly Jominian. Almost daily, technology gains in importance, and although officers speak of embracing chaos, or of allowing more freedom to their subordinates, their words do not reflect the reality of the current situation. *Auftragstaktik* is far more than Mission Command. Without necessary preconditions, it cannot be conceptually grafted, easily or otherwise, from Germany into a multinational alliance. Although NATO Alliance members can certainly learn from the German experience, they cannot incorporate a leadership philosophy that is almost two centuries old by merely changing its name and inserting it into their manuals. Unless the receiving militaries are willing to restructure their entire organizations, reconsider what their leaders believe to be most important in battle, revamp their educational systems from basic training to their staff colleges, and formally incorporate general staffs, then these countries must accept that this borrowing experiment is doomed from the outset. This book demonstrates why.

Although Mission Command has been adopted as one of the building blocks of a newly re-invigorated Alliance-wide doctrine, was it realistic to expect that NATO countries could successfully import *Auftragstaktik*? There is no simple answer, but the likelihood of the successful transposition, of the 'conceptual grafting' of *Auftragstaktik* into any foreign military is slim, and incorporating it into a multinational alliance, arguably even more so. This book demonstrates that *Auftragstaktik* remains merely the tip of a doctrinal iceberg. Seen holistically, *Auftragstaktik* encompasses many diverse aspects of the military profession. It includes military theory, the command climate, the educational process, the structure of the military and the society that the military springs from and serves. The reality of most NATO countries in general, and of Canada, Great Britain, and the United States in particular, is that *Auftragstaktik* cannot simply be plucked from the *Bundeswehr* and then grafted onto current Anglo-Saxon leadership philosophies.

✠ ✠ ✠

Before continuing, a word or two on what is *German* and what is *Prussian* is in order. In Germany, there is an almost universal understanding of what it means to be German and culturally, this understanding ignores national borders. In many other countries across Europe, there are communities and aspects of German culture extant from Switzerland to the Baltic and from Alsace to Hungary. They may not be German nationals but, culturally, there is no doubt about who they are. For instance, in the 1990s, a newly re-unified Germany 'repatriated' over a million ethnic Germans from Russia and all over the ex-USSR, instantly recognizing them as German and giving them citizenship – even though some of their families had been away from the Fatherland since the 18th century. This immediate recognition did not sit well with the millions of non-German immigrants whose families may have been in Germany for several generations and still not been given citizenship. Further, within this concept of German culture, the term Prussian is held as a unique sub-culture and not always seen favourably by all members of German society (particularly so in Bavaria). Thus, the term *German* is not as straightforward as what might be thought to a non-German. Whether it is respect for authority, a unique work ethic or something as simple as the German belief that *Ordnung ist ein halb des Lebens*, that good order is half of life, it is not a simple matter of national boundaries. It is cultural.

The time span covered in this study is a period during which Prussia, as well as being a sovereign state, eventually took control of a confederation of small German political entities and forged them, using Bismarck's words, by blood and iron, into the modern state of Germany. In order to avoid a socio-political dissertation on the difference between what is Prussian and what is German, *Prussia* is used primarily when the point being made is related to a historical context. *Germany* is used either for the period after unification in 1871, or more broadly in relation to something cultural or pan-Germanic. Likewise, most of the early history is drawn primarily from the Prussian tradition and situation. The state of affairs in Baden, Württemberg, Hesse, Saxony *et al* are not extensively examined since they tended to follow the Prussian lead –Bavaria being a notable exception.

Finally, the complex social development of the officer corps is not considered in any great detail. The development and practices of German officers is well covered elsewhere and is both highly complex and controversial. But one aspect of German military leadership is not controversial. Since German officers had a unique relationship with their society, their sovereign, and their soldiers, they stood out amongst all their European peers. Their leadership was unique. Born of a small and impoverished duchy, this uniqueness eventually flowered into a system of battlefield leadership that stood above all other militaries. It was leadership in ways that were at once commonsensical and paradoxical. It was *Enlightened Leadership*.

NOTES

[1] Although this book focuses primarily upon the German Army (*Bundesheer*), the term *Bundeswehr* (Armed Forces) is often used whenever the issue has a national impact greater than just what concerns the ground forces. Also, within the *Bundeswehr*, the army has always had an overwhelming dominance over the other two services and so what applied to the army almost invariably applied to the two smaller services.

[2] The *Wehrmacht* was the name of the German armed forces during the Nazi period. It is mistakenly but commonly used to refer principally to the army. The army has always used its traditional name of *Heer*. Before the Nazi period, it was the *Reichsheer*, and before that it was the *Kaiserheer*; now it is the *Bundesheer*. To further complicate the issue, under the Nazis the *Waffen SS* did not belong to the *Wehrmacht* but was under its tactical command and used most of the *Wehrmacht*'s tactical doctrine. Writers often, and mistakenly, use the *Waffen SS* as examples of *Wehrmacht* tactical prowess.

[3] The General Staff and the Great General Staff were the same organization. (Confusingly the Quartermaster Staff concerned itself with supplies and was mostly non-military, but the *Generalquartiermeister* was the deputy to the *Chef der Generalstab*.) General Karl *Freiherr* von Müffling instituted the name change in 1821 while he was Chief of the General Staff. The renaming to Great General Staff assisted in differentiating the central staff from the staffs of the various army Corps, all of which were called General Staffs. See **Chapter 2** and **Annex B**. Further, the term General Staff can become a bit confusing. Once it came into use, it described both the group of officers at the Royal Headquarters and the handful of officers in a field formation such as an infantry Division or an army Corps. Strictly speaking, the General Staffs in the field army were called *Truppen Generalstab* but for simplicity they are all referred to here by their generic title. Thus, there was a Chief of General Staff in Berlin as well as Chief of General Staff in each field formation. Naturally, The Chief of the General Staff was the one at the Royal Headquarters in Berlin.

[4] The use of "von" in German names can be confusing for non-German readers. This is especially true for those individuals, like Graf von Scharnhorst, who were ennobled late in life. In many cases in the book the 'von' is used intermittently, which is often how it is used in German.

Arminius
Illustration by August Tholey, 1894

KRIEGSKUNST

The greatest disgrace that can befall them is to have abandoned their shields.
- Tacitus, AD 98

rom Arminius' destruction of three Roman Legions, *Legio XVII, Legio XVIII and Legio XIX*, over the course of four days at the Teutoberg Forest in 9 C.E. to the *Blitzkrieg* victories of the *Wehrmacht* at the beginning of the Second World War, much has been written on the Germans and their fighting abilities. Disregarding the spurious notion that the Germans were somehow more warlike than other nations, one is left to wonder whether these abilities were the result of unique structures, tactics, and capabilities. Some authors, like Trevor Dupuy and Martin van Creveld, have cited the Great General Staff as the root of Germany's battlefield excellence. Interestingly, this opinion is also the official view of the current *Bundeswehr* as manifested in its curriculum at its *FüAk* in Hamburg. Certainly, a key factor that has had an enduring influence on Germany's history has been its need for strong military forces, necessitated by its geographical location of being at the crossroads of Central Europe while also often trapped among hostile neighbours. Whatever the reasons for Germany's battlefield renown, one thing was certain: the Germans, in Dupuy's words, surely have demonstrated "a genius for war."

The first step in gaining a better understanding of *Auftragstaktik*, must be to appreciate the unique development

13

of German *Kriegskunst* or Art of War. In this chapter the investigation will trace the major trends and developments during the two and a half centuries separating the arrival of the Great Elector Frederick Wilhelm in 1640 and that of Kaiser Wilhelm II in 1888. The chapter will follow the *leitmotif* of armed conflict and the invariably formative events in the evolution of Prusso-German warfare, both in methodology and in philosophy. In this way, we will explore and evaluate how and why Prusso-German *Kriegskunst* became, and then remained, unique.

Throughout history, many nations have developed their own philosophies, styles, or schools of warfare. The Macedonians fought differently than did the Persians. The medieval Swiss fought differently from their contemporary Italian neighbours. In modern times, the British way of war has been distinctly different from the American, as both were from the German. This fact raises the obvious question: Why was this so? What factors came into play to cause one national group to develop a method of making war, which was different from its neighbours, associates, and enemies? Was it a matter of geography? Was it a question of culture? Was it merely a chance of history? As eminent historians like Edward Gibbon, William H. McNeill and Paul Kennedy have demonstrated in their respective works, nations and civilizations rise and fall as if on a tide. European history has been an ever-changing mosaic of waxing and waning militaristic dynasties. If it were true that certain nations were predisposed toward militarism, then it would also hold that these nations would exercise hegemony for very long periods of time. But this is not the case. Medieval Swiss mercenaries were the best that money could buy in their time. Eventually, they gave way to Italian *Condottieri*. They in turn were defeated by the Spanish *tercios* that were later shattered by Gustavus Adolphus and his Swedish armies. Frederick the Great was the master of the battlefield in his day, as was Napoleon Bonaparte after Frederick's passing. Clearly, any argument based purely on cultural proclivity is false.

When viewed through the long lens of history, an interesting commonality emerges: All of Europe's armies developed along similar, parallel tracks. If national cultures and the vagaries of fortune were the only factors in the development of the various schools of warfare in Europe, then they would all have developed the same way. Not surprisingly, for generations, this is exactly what happened. Discounting the highs and the lows, which the Great Captains brought to their respective nations, warfare in one country was what it was in another – almost. There was one outlier: Prussia. For centuries it followed a parallel path to all its neighbours, then in the middle of 17th century the Margraviate of Brandenburg, one of the primary constituent states of the Holy Roman Empire since 1157, took an unexpected turn and began the evolution of the Prusso-German School of war. A military progression that for centuries had been much like its counterparts in England, France, or Russia, somehow became unique. And it was not merely a matter of size or weapons, for as many historians have noted, Prussia was distinctive from its neighbours not so much in degree as in kind.

Consider for a moment an analogy from the science of chemistry. One could create a supersaturated solution, which so long as it was left undisturbed, could lay in stasis indefinitely. Some sort of catalyst would be needed to precipitate some new compound. The Prussian army, in its deeply entrenched feudal forms, could have remained an effective fighting force and never attained uniqueness. A catalytic event was required that would alter the path of the Prussian view of warfare and, this is exactly what occurred.

When one looks at modern Germany, it is easy to forget that this nation in the heart of Europe was not always the economic and military powerhouse that it eventually became:

[The lands] of the Electorate of Brandenburg, stitched together by a random process of inheritance, sprawling discontinuously and defencelessly across the German plain from the Vistula to the Rhine, could not compare in terms of natural wealth even with the neighbouring lands of Saxony and Bavaria.... Moreover, they contained some of the most stubbornly independent towns and insubordinate nobility in Europe. It was difficult enough to persuade the suspicious representatives of these Estates to provide money for forces even for local defence, let alone for conflicts which the Elector might have to fight at the other end of his domains. Whatever they did, it might have been confidently predicted that the Hohenzollerns simply could not win; against their own subjects, let alone anyone else.[1]

The slow and methodical rise to power by the House of Hohenzollern, beginning in 1415 and lasting until the abdication of Wilhelm II in 1918, was not part of some multi-generational, well-executed, plan. Invariably, each progressive step was the result of one dire immediate need or another. But that is not to denigrate the considerable abilities of the ruling family. Like the de Medici in Italy, the Hohenzollerns produced a line of unusually astute and capable men. This was critical, for after the ruinous Thirty Years' War (1618-1648) there was a great and undoubted need for leadership. The Peace of Westphalia had left the German states in near-ruinous turmoil. Casualties had been catastrophic. Some areas of Europe saw depopulation of almost three quarters! Into this chaos "the active policy of the Brandenburg electors of the House of Hohenzollern fell like a stone into a stagnant pool."[2]

The reality of the post-war Brandenburg Margraviate was that no political achievement was possible without the control of a well-functioning army and Elector Frederick Wilhelm, did not have one. Brandenburg gained several territories in the Treaty of Westphalia (1648), but the Elector's territories were both devastated and far-flung. Thus, possessing both a weakened and nearly destroyed realm, from necessity, he immediately set about to rebuild both his army and his holdings. At first, his army comprised little more than a collection of dishonest and unreliable mercenaries whom he soon dismissed. Raising armies required cash and that was something else the elector lacked. Being clever, he soon stumbled upon a solution. To raise a small army to fight in one of the recurring Baltic wars, the Great Elector promised his difficult Estates General, his suspicious and insubordinate landed nobles, that he would confirm all their existing privileges in exchange for a grant of money. They quickly agreed. Although none could have imagined it, this agreement proved to be the first step on the road to an absolutist Prussian monarchy. In modern parlance, he co-opted them and in so doing, laid the foundations of a system that inextricably linked all Prussian noble families to the Hohenzollern family and thence to royal service.

Having received the money to raise a force, Frederick Wilhelm immediately built a standing army. Starting with a mere 3,000 men in 1640, within four decades, he was able to field an army of over 40,000 men. This force came from a rather impoverished society of only some two million subjects. To his contemporaries, the elector's army was a force with which to be reckoned – both internally and throughout Europe. In 1654, for example, the Holy Roman Emperor, Leopold I, urged all inhabitants of the empire to support their various princes. Frederick Wilhelm seized upon this instruction as the moral imperative for his actions – although most imperial edicts until then had been routinely ignored. Having now both the legal and the moral impetus to use his new force, he did so with impunity against any of his holdings and nobles recalcitrant in paying their taxes. The new army soon brought Frederick Wilhelm onto the greater European stage. In 1675, his army repelled a Swedish invasion at Fehrbellin, thereby establishing Brandenburg as a military power.

Concurrent with the building of his army, the Great Elector created a system of royal officials, which was ostensibly introduced to help in the war effort, but soon became permanently ensconced in the various communities to extend his royal economic control:

> In the towns, where the money was found by an excise on goods, they extended their control over all the industrial and commercial activities. In the countryside they extended a similar supervision over harvests, rents, and general taxation. Like the French intendants, these Prussian officials, the *Steuerkommissäre* and *Landräthe,* created a bureaucratic framework which gave the crown a new degree of control over the economic activities and resources of its subjects and

which gradually eliminating local rights and particularisms, produced an effective central government focused on Berlin. A State, in fact: the Prussian State, called into being to provide for the needs of the King of Prussia's army.[3]

However, this web of bureaucrats alone was not enough to ensure that the wide-ranging holdings could be welded together. There had to be more. The army had to become both capable and reliable. The disparate and discontinuous lands between Cleve, on the Dutch border, Ravensberg, Brandenburg, and Prussia in the far east had no natural links that brought them together. That they were forged into a viable political union, which became recognized as a European power, was the result of the skill of the Hohenzollern rulers and the effectiveness of their growing military. An effective army needed equally effective leadership. To this end, the next step in making the newly conglomerated state work competently was an officer corps that could be relied upon to do the king's bidding. The crown found the answer to its dilemma in the impoverished but arrogant *Junkers* of Prussia.

> The officers were found almost exclusively from the nobility, who were virtually conscripted to the royal service – noble families being compelled to send one son into the cadet corps from which the mainstream of officers was drawn. In return for a confirmation of all their privileges, the Prussian nobility were bound to the services of the crown. Within a couple of generations, a *noblesse* which rivalled their neighbours the Poles in their wild and unbiddable independence had become the docile pillars of the Hohenzollern monarchy...[4]

It was not as easy as simply ordering the nobility to provide officers for the army. There had to be some sort of impetus for the noble families to offer up their sons for royal service. Astutely, the Hohenzollerns understood this requirement. Simply put, the incentives for the *Junker* class were two-fold. The first was social. Army officers were awarded social status by the king, who raised his officers above all other nobility merely by making them all brother military officers to himself. They all wore the so-called 'King's Coat'. By decree, the officer corps became an insulated and protected class within society. They were ultimately answerable only to the monarch. The second incentive was an expression of power, and thereby of wealth. From the 17th century until the Kaiser's abdication, for all intents and purposes, all Prussian officers served not the state, but the monarch personally.[5] The result was an officer corps that was both personally and intimately linked to the sovereign. This had the effect of making the Prussian officer corps one of the most socially exclusive élites in Europe, and the Hohenzollerns worked hard to keep it so; partly in fulfillment of a social compact, partly because they placed great store in the aristocratic code of honour and loyalty, thereby ensuring subservience to almost any royal whim.

Despite the formative changes made by the Great Elector, and maintained by his son Frederick I, the poverty-stricken Brandenburg holdings were not yet fully knit together nor free of foreign debt. The Great Elector's grandson, Frederick Wilhelm I, achieved the next great accomplishment when he created the canton system. This system allowed his army regiments the exclusive rights to recruit within well-defined geographic boundaries as well as establishing a rudimentary form of obligatory service. Although Frederick Wilhelm I did establish a sound financial basis for his realm, there is little of real interest with respect to the development of a unique fighting force except that he, like Philip of Macedon before him, established all the preconditions that would allow his son, another Frederick, to grasp the reins of power and continue to expand the family holdings. Unfortunately for the king, his son the crown prince showed almost no interest in things martial, and it drove Frederick Wilhelm I to near despair.

Crown Prince Frederick not only did not seem interested in military matters, he seemed also to spurn the German language and its people, preferring French culture, language, philosophy, and the arts. Beginning in 1736, Prince Frederick began a longstanding correspondence with the great French *philosophe* Voltaire, beginning a friendship that ended only with Voltaire's death in 1778. In fact, upon becoming king, the language of his Prussian royal court, like its name – *Sanssouci* – was French and, not long after his ascension to the throne, he created an exclusive new order of merit for personal achievement, a *Verdienstorden*, which he named in French, *Pour le Mérite*, many of which were in later years awarded to German officers for fighting against the French!

The young Frederick had a difficult and unhappy childhood and in return was a difficult son. At 18, he attempted to escape his tyrannical father but was captured and imprisoned for almost two years under a suspended sentence of death. After his imprisonment, Frederick eventually reconciled with his father. Although Frederick was only 21, his father made him a colonel and the head of an infantry regiment and sent him to war under the command of Prince Eugene of Savoy. At this time Frederick began to see both the importance of a strong army and that he himself had not insignificant skills in this field.

Frederick Wilhelm I died on 31 May 1740 and his son took the throne as Frederick II. Later that same year, Charles VI of Austria, Holy Roman Emperor, died and was succeeded as ruler of Austria by his daughter Maria Theresa, the only Habsburg female to rule their vast holdings. Within two months of Maria Theresa ascending to the throne, the newly enthroned and once anti-military Frederick II, seeing and seizing an opportunity, invaded Silesia, Austria's richest province. By the spring of the following year, France, Spain, Bavaria, and Saxony all joined Prussia in attacking Austria, which started the War of Austrian Succession. That year Prussia defeated Austria and kept Silesia as a spoil of war. So began the birth of the modern German military.

Frederick II, soon to be known to the world as Frederick the Great, made some important military innovations in terms of infantry tactics, rigid discipline, battlefield manoeuvre, and even propaganda. Most importantly, the once reluctant prince and new king took the army he inherited and used it with astounding effect. Through a combination of innate military talent and political ambition, he was able to wield the power of his army, as his ancestors had done, to strengthen Prussia. His leadership and tactical genius are well-documented and inspired many great soldiers including Napoleon, but what is perhaps less-well appreciated is Frederick's political astuteness. Frederick was more than just the king. He strongly reinforced the already well-established Prussian tradition that the king was not only the first *citizen* of the realm; he was also the first *soldier* of the state.

Alas for Prussia, Frederick the Great's military genius and political brilliance died with him. Although a great battlefield commander and an astute political leader, Frederick must bear a great deal of responsibility for the fate that befell his kingdom after his death. He and his father had built the Prussian army into the most formidable military machine in Europe, but Frederick did little to extend its strength beyond his own reign. He did not invest in modernization nor in the development of his army's skills, remaining content to rest upon the laurels he had won on the battlefield. Even before his death, the Prussian army was already beginning to decline and moving inexorably towards its own catastrophic collapse, a downfall that Frederick himself predicted. With no children of his own, he knew that his realm would pass to his nephew Frederick Wilhelm, about whom the uncle had no illusions, foretelling of how his successor would ultimately spend the state treasury on his court and allow the army to waste away. Yet Frederick did nothing to prevent his prediction from being fulfilled.

The dual calamity that befell post-Frederician Prussia was one of the unfortunate coincidences of history. Concurrent with Frederick the Great's death in 1786, the European political climate turned unusually dangerous. The political turmoil into which Europe fell because of the French Revolution is too complex to be unravelled here. In simple terms, the death of the Great Frederick, at a time when the country needed a strong leader, left Prussia in weak, inexpert hands. Frederick's nephew, both wasteful and incompetent, took the throne as Frederick Wilhelm II and through ineptitude and indolence proceeded to fulfil his uncle's dire prophecies of him. Although he oversaw some minor legal reforms, he also became enmeshed in a war with France as well as the two Partitions of Poland. By the time of his death in 1797, Prussia was nearly irredeemably in debt and the country's nobles were increasingly taking power away from the crown. Frederick Wilhelm II's reign had reversed nearly a century of consolidation of both the Prussian treasury and of its ruling family.

Frederick Wilhelm II was succeeded in turn by his son, the timorous Frederick Wilhelm III. Sadly, for the country, neither father nor son had inherited any of their uncle's military genius. Wielding the great and complex military machine that had been forged by their ancestors was beyond both of their meagre abilities. Both the nephew and the great-nephew had neither the foresight nor the desire to reform either the decaying Prussian state or the somnolent military. Further, they both lacked the abilities required to govern the bureaucracy, which the Great Frederick had intentionally kept firmly in his own two hands. When this decay and lack of ruling ability combined with the formidable abilities and territorial ambitions of Napoleon, the resulting ineptitude led to the disintegration of the complex and once powerful Prussian state. All that awaited them was the deathblow to be struck by the French army, for "in the fields of diplomacy, defence, administration and social life the state machine worked with complacent incompetence which even by 18th century standards was remarkable."[6] The end was clearly in sight:

> A defeat in these circumstances was almost inevitable. What caused the greatest surprise both to friend and to foe was the complete collapse of the Prussian Army after the brave and bloody fight which it had put up on the battlefields of Jena and Auerstädt.... The strongholds of the Prussian state fell, one after the other, without resistance, handed over by their weak and incompetent commanders.... The rest of the war, after this catastrophic beginning, could only postpone the inevitable end.[7]

Ironically, the dual defeat of Jena and Auerstädt was a catalytic first step in making the Prussian army once again the envy of Europe. It would prove to be a long climb back to the top.

From humble beginnings, the Prussian monarchy,

intentionally or otherwise, had set about forging a multi-layered union. The first layer was a coalition of disparate and physically divided lands. The second was the establishment of a professional army that would grow to become the desideratum of all Europe. The last was an officer corps inextricably bound to the monarchy and, more particularly, to the personal will of the king. Beginning with the Great Elector, Prussia held its army in distinctive high regard. For the next two centuries, unlike in most of the rest of Europe, the feudal concept of personal fealty to an omnipotent monarch was held in stasis in Prussia. In fact, beginning with Frederick the Great, the feudal bond between the officer corps and the king was continually strengthened. How the monarchy accomplished all of this was straightforward: The Hohenzollerns used the army as a binding element, which held monarch and military fast to one another. In fact, some historians have even argued that there never really was a Prussian nation *per se*. There was only the state of Prussia and its army. Or as Voltaire reputedly said: Whilst most states have an army the Prussian army has a state.

Frederick the Great had developed the army to be not only the school of the nation, but also a formidable nation-building force and, even in decline, the army was able to maintain a strong enough tradition to ensure both its own survival and its continued predominance in Prussian and German society. It is well to remember, however, that the relationship between a state and its military is unique to each culture. Prussia demonstrated a civil-military relationship altogether different from those in either Britain or France, for instance. In Prussia, this relationship had remained decidedly feudal, cut off from the social reforms in the remainder of Europe. The court martial of artillery captain Alfred Dreyfus in France brought the civil-military relationship under fierce scrutiny, eventually acting as a watershed for future developments in this relationship. In contrast, a similar accusation of a naval cadet in England during the same period went almost unnoticed by English society.

Not all the consequences of the feudal ties between the army and the monarchy were positive. One of the negative effects was the retarding of Prussia's nascent liberal democracy. Like most of its European neighbours in the 19th century, Prussia along with all the other German states, was undergoing social and political upheaval. To appreciate the environment within which the army existed, it is therefore necessary to have some understanding of the civil-military relationship within Prussia and greater Germany.

For the Prussian army to properly play its powerful role necessitated unique circumstances. Whether by design or accident of history, these circumstances existed in 19th century Prussia. Armies do not exist in isolation; they are products of the societies that create them. They therefore exhibit, to greater or lesser degrees, the same prejudices, concerns, and beliefs as the societies from which they spring. Unlike the Austrian Empire, which was far more ethnically diverse than Prussia and other German neighbours, Prussian society in the 19th century was relatively homogeneous both culturally and linguistically. The Prussian army was likewise so. Under Prussian leadership, the evolving political structure, that after 1871 became the Greater German *Reich,* was little more than a territorial extension of old Prussia, with the Prussian king as the new German *Kaiser*. The form of government and the subsequent workings of that government were therefore understandably Prussian in outlook, attitude, and demeanour.

Prussia was not as advanced in its embrace of the Industrial Revolution as many of its neighbours, but by the second half of the 19th century, Prussia had become a full and influential member of the industrial group of European nations. The advancements made by the *Zollverein*, a customs union, to some extent went beyond reducing petty tariffs and increasing trade. To a limited degree, the *Zollverein* worked to spread liberal political ideologies. Prussia had finally crawled out of her poverty and had successfully carved out a respected niche in the European political order. The country had a relatively stable system of government, was prospering and with the increased investment in the national infrastructure of roads, railways, and schools, the country was beginning to make great social and economic strides. The age-old relationships among church, monarchy, and society, even if under siege by the waves of liberalism that had swept Europe during the previous half century, were stable. Prussian militarism, which was the product of generations of tradition and history, worked in concert with the bureaucracy to maintain social order and national security.

Although the French Revolution had an impact upon Prussia, the socially volatile ideals of *liberté, fraternité,* and *égalité* did not take hold there as they had done in France. The political fallout of the French Revolution with its removal of the monarchy and the rise of Napoleon was the eventual dissolution of the Holy Roman Empire. The multitude of German states, both great and small, were cut adrift and went through several confederations and alliances during this period, beginning in 1803 with the *Reichsdeputationshauptschluss.* By 1806, the year Napoleon smashed the Holy Roman Empire, these associations had evolved into the *Rheinbund.*

Although behind England and France in accepting social change, Germany was not immune to these forces. First in the *Rheinbund* states, and thereafter in Prussia, reformers called for the abolition of serfdom, the dissolution of feudal barriers to trade, and the creation of a free and responsible citizenry. The German princes, as heirs of absolute power, were loath to grant their citizens these demands. Only hesitantly did some of the south German princes grant their states their own constitutions. The defeat of Napoleon, and the subsequent Congress of Vienna in 1815, did little to appease the wishes of those wanting to create a Greater Germany. The creation of the *Deutscher Bund* saw only a loosely formed association of member states within which little could be accomplished unless the two largest states, Prussia and Austria – and critically important, the longest-standing rivals for dominance – agreed. With generations of animosity between the Hohenzollerns and the Habsburgs, such agreement was not likely. Thus, the liberal movement suffered under the *Bund.* The German press continued to be constrained; universities were closely watched and political agitation was virtually impossible. Except for the creation of the *Zollverein*, there was little real gain made in German society by the liberal movement between the Congress of Vienna in 1815 and the revolutionary movements of 1848. Following the Prussian lead in 1818, most of the German states had repealed their internal tariffs and, again under Prussian dominance, the *Zollverein* exercised leadership in pan-German activity.

In 1848, Europe experienced another wave of social unrest. This time the German states joined in and their surprised princes were obliged to grant their subjects some concessions. A national assembly was called in Frankfurt am Main and the Liberal Centre political bloc carried the day. Yet, the assembly was splintered. Once again, the two great powers within the German Confederacy could not agree. Prussia and Austria remained at odds. A constitution excluding Austria was drawn up and the hereditary Holy Roman imperial crown offered to the Prussian king, but Frederick Wilhelm IV declined to dignify the rabble of a revolution by adding Prussian majesty to the mix. Along with his refusal, came the withdrawal of Prussian support to the assembly. Austria having already withdrawn, the other German princes followed suit and by 1849 the assembly was dead and so, too, was the German liberal movement.

Prussian liberalism had placed its hopes in their liberal-minded king but the unexpected illness of Frederick Wilhelm IV in 1857 and the ascendancy to the throne of his brother Wilhelm, a despot and dedicated professional army officer, put a halt to any inroads which Prussian liberals may have made among the ranks of the officer corps. Beginning as prince regent and continuing as king and later as *Kaiser*, Wilhelm's priorities lay in rebuilding and strengthening his army at the expense of internal political reform. The new king was having difficulty raising funds to expand his military, but he soon found a solution. He appointed *Prinz* Otto von Bismarck to the post of *Ministerpräsident* in 1862. Bismarck, both astute and respected, quelled the troublesome House of Deputies, thereby assuring Wilhelm's vision for an even more militarized Prussia.

Wilhelm's manoeuvrings did not go unnoticed abroad. In England, his grandmother, Queen Victoria, grew concerned about her awkward and militarily obsessed grandson. To make matters worse, it was not long before it became obvious that Bismarck had plans of his own. It became evident that the Minister President was seeking a confrontation with Prussia's oldest and greatest rival, Austria. Bismarck sought not just a politically unified Germany; he sought a unified Germany under the autocratic Prussian monarchy. Under the combined influence of Wilhelm and Bismarck, democratic reform was never allowed to take root. The great upheavals and advances made in the liberal movements throughout most of Europe of 1848-49, and again in the 1860s, made very little impact upon Prussia. Thus, despite growing and manifold protestations for democratic reform throughout the 19th century, Prussia, and after 1871, the *Reich*, under Prussian control, never developed an empowered electorate to the same degree as did the more liberal democracies of England and France.

Not everyone saw these events as unfortunate. From the army's perspective, the professional soldier's unexpected ascendancy to the throne had happily stopped all liberal influence in its tracks. The generations of *Junkers*, who had sent sons to the army, had been alarmed at the liberal waves sweeping Europe. Any attempts to modernize the nation or 'their' army were seen as anathema. Wilhelm agreed with his nobles and saw any reforms as attempts to weaken the feudal links that kept Prussian society functioning and were therefore strongly rebuffed. The centuries-old feudal relationships among the army, the monarchy, and the state suited both Wilhelm and Bismarck, so progress in this sphere lagged well behind the rest of Europe. When this lack of liberal democratic grounding combined with the proud military traditions and technical innovations of the Prussian military, a special civil-military relationship emerged. Most dramatically, this relationship manifested itself in the workings of a growing sub-culture of military professionals – *der Großen Generalstab*, the Great General Staff.

In purely military terms, the Great General Staff was the brains and the governing body of the army. Both in peace and in war, it selected, trained, and employed only the brightest and most capable officers, forming them into a closely-knit and homogeneous body of men. Like all officers, these select men were sworn to defend the country but personally, like their forefathers, they owed their allegiance not to the state, but to the personage of the king himself. Highly successful, much admired, and widely copied, the Great General Staff came to epitomize institutional brilliance in all things martial. Britain, France, Italy, Russia, Japan and even the United States all copied the General Staff system to improve their own armies. What they were not able to recreate, however, was the unique independence of the *Generalstab* from all the other organs of state. Stability remained the watchword of Prussian militarism. Social change was denounced by this ancient military culture. The canton system which Frederick Wilhelm I had created in 1733 continued to function; but, by the end of the century, the recruitment system, along with the other internal systems of the army, needed reform and needed it badly.

For generations, the Prussian army had avoided universal conscription. The French Revolution had raised the spectre of a nation in arms, and the *levées en masse* of Napoleon now made the matter more urgent. At the turn of the century, Gerhard David von Scharnhorst, chief among the reformers and a senior member of the General Staff, saw great advantages in the French method. He repeatedly raised the issue but to no avail. The Prussian army had yet to experience any large-scale defeat and those who continued to see the army as invincible carried the day – until 1806.

The French Revolution was a watershed historical event. It changed Europe and arguably, the world. The subsequent rise of Napoleon and his eponymous wars changed not just the face of Europe but the ways that wars were fought. And nowhere was this change in warfare more pronounced than in Prussia. The shattering defeat of the Prussians at the battles of Jena and Auerstädt in 1806 brought an end to Prussia's complacency and offered a new beginning for some of the reform-minded officers who had warned of impending doom.

The Prussian army, built by Frederick the Great but

practically unused for decades, had fallen into a terrible state of neglect. Still convinced of its battlefield superiority, which had been earned under the command of Frederick, the army took to the field in 1806 confident that it could beat the French. Nothing could have been further from the truth. The French army had better leadership, superior numbers, and newer tactics. On the Prussian side, command of the combined armies was exercised through a council of war whereas on the French side Napoleon commanded the campaign personally. The individual skills of the Prussian infantry were abysmal, and commanders soon realized that they needed to break off the engagement. The French, through superior tempo, surprised the Prussians during their battlefield withdrawal. Napoleon's skill combined with Prussian ineptness and a violent attack by the Imperial Guards and the cavalry turned a retreat into a full rout. The Battle of Jena was a textbook example of French mobility and the use of reserves to reinforce success. There was nothing left for the Prussians to do but to surrender. Europe sat stunned by the Prussian loss and even Napoleon saw the significance of the victory, making a special pilgrimage to Frederick the Great's tomb to celebrate his win.

In 1807, after the punitive Treaty of Tilsit, the Prussian king, initially reluctant, finally agreed that the army needed reform and appointed a commission. Scharnhorst, as the head of the commission, pressed home his views calling for a mass mobilization of the entire people like the French *levées en masse*. Many senior members of the army supported him, but the commission was opposed by most of the *Junker* officers and so initial progress was faltering. Some improvements were made, but the debate on conscription was brought to a head by new conflict and the renewed universal *levées* of France. None-the-less, Scharnhorst's appeals to the king fell upon deaf ears.

Although Scharnhorst lost his fight to create a nation in arms, the other reforms that he instituted as head of the Reform Commission were far more significant. The officer corps was opened to men of talent, irrespective of birth. New tactics were adopted. The brutal punishments instituted by

Frederick the Great were removed or lessened. The French structures of brigades, divisions and corps were incorporated. Most importantly, the early steps taken in the formation of a true General Staff were solidified and formalized. This last step was to be the most propitious. Although Scharnhorst did not live to see the defeat of Napoleon or the rise of the Prussian School of warfare, the formative first steps were taken by him and brought to fruition by his successor August von Gneisenau. Taking the helm after Scharnhorst's death from wounds of in 1813, Gneisenau introduced the concept of working from directives instead of rigid orders. This idea was called *Führen durch Auftrag*, or leading by directive, and would one day grow to become *Auftragstaktik*. The reformers put the Prussian army on a new road to military excellence and, as a group, they dragged Prussia out of the previous century and built the foundation that would allow it to face an uncertain future. In so doing, they broke not only with the immediate past but also with the rest of Europe.

By the time of Napoleon's defeat at Waterloo in 1815, the ideological schism between the Prussian way of war and all others was complete. The Napoleonic Wars had fundamentally disrupted Prussia, and the Prussian army. The French had been led by a military genius not seen since Julius Caesar. The English were secure in the belief that they could continue to create future leaders on the playing fields of Eton. However, the Prussians, having had two bad monarchs in succession, realized that they could not count on the appearance of genius to save them. Therefore, the road down which they went was one of institutionalizing military excellence as embodied in their General Staff. The Prussian General Staff was composed of men who shared a common view of warfare and philosophy of combat. In peace, they planned for war. In war, they were the touchstone of tactical excellence for the army at all levels. Apart from running the army, their duty was also to review critically, and evaluate, all major campaigns and battles to determine not only what had gone right, but more importantly, what had gone wrong. They were the embodiment of the Prussian way of war.

Specially selected, and highly trained, they were *la crème de la crème,* and as such they guided the creation of a unique school of warfare – a unique Prussian *Kriegskunst.*

At the post-First World War peace talks in 1919, the Allies blamed the Great General Staff for causing the war and, therefore, outlawed the organization. By forcing Germany to give up her most powerful military tool, the victors expected to cripple Germany's ability to wage any future wars. The fundamental Allied misunderstanding, however, was in believing that the General Staff was the culprit for, as subsequent academic research has shown, the causes of the First World War were far more complex than the militarism of the General Staff. But in one respect the Allied officers were correct. The Staff was more than merely the governing body of the army. It was the physical manifestation of a unique view of warfare – *Kriegskunst* – a form that proudly traced its lineage back to the Great Elector.

✠ ✠ ✠

In Clausewitzian terms, the uniqueness of *Kriegskunst* can be viewed on two planes. The physical plane saw the development of tactics and techniques by men such as Frederick the Great. These physical manifestations, such as precision drill and iron discipline, were in themselves reason enough to have made the Prussian army an exceptional and formidable fighting force. The battlefield expertise accumulated by the Prussians was most impressive-but, as imposing as this expertise was, it proved to be fleeting and in the end was insufficient to withstand the martial genius of Napoleon. The Prussian contributions to the art of war went beyond the physical. The truly significant and lasting changes in *Kriegskunst* were developed on the moral plane: Accentuation of the military as a profession; total dedication to the study of the substance rather than merely the trappings of war; and the practice of warfare that emphasized independent thought and action within the framework of a superior's concept – *Auftragstaktik* – were but a few of the many innovations that separated the Prussians, and by extension the Germans, from their neighbours and their adversaries.

The creation of the first true General Staff by the Prussians was a watershed development in warfare. In formally instituting this body of men to provide the king with an instrument of statecraft, the Prussians laid the foundation for the modification of war as Europe knew it. Despite its uniqueness, the great utility of this advancement was not merely its creation. More important was its implementation. By the time storm clouds were gathering again over Europe at the end of the 19th century, the Great General Staff, with its independent power and influence, was the product of the evolution of almost two centuries of growth, development, and nurturing. From its tenuous beginnings in Brandenburg, through the era of Frederician Prussia, and revitalized during the catastrophe that created the Reform Commission of 1807, the welding together of the feudal officer corps and the concept of a General Staff, had results out of all proportion to the mere sum of the individual parts. Alone, any of the singular aspects of technical expertise, historical development, feudal ties within the officer corps, or individual brilliance of staff officers, could not possibly have created the Prusso-German school of war. Taken as a whole, however, the combination created a startling synergy. Like a jigsaw puzzle that is merely bits of paper until it is pieced together, the manifold components of the German military experience combined to create a new and lasting view of human conflict. Most significantly, the marriage of a feudal officer corps to the dual concepts of a General Staff and independent action – *Auftragstaktik* – produced the unexpected genius of Prusso-German *Kriegskunst*.

NOTES

[1] Michael Howard, *War in European History*, (Oxford, 1976), pp. 66-7. Note that electors were below the rank of king but were monarchs in their own right; they were so named because mid-way through the 12th century, the ruler had been given the title Kurfürst or Elector and had been given the right to cast a vote to elect the Holy Roman Emperor.

[2] Herbert Rosinski, *The German Army*, (Washington DC, 1944), p.10.

[3] Howard, *European History*, p 69.

[4] *Ibid*, p. 69-70.

[5] It was this centuries-old tradition of a medieval relationship of fealty to the leader that allowed Adolf Hitler to force his officers to swear an oath of allegiance to him personally. Notably, modern *Bundeswehr* officers swear their oath of loyalty to *"das deutsche Volk"* (the German people). See Ceremonial Oath Sworn by *Bundeswehr* Officers and NCOs in the Epilogue.

[6] Walter Görlitz, *History of the German General Staff 1657-1945*. Translated by Brian Battershaw, (New York, 1961), p 16.

[7] Rosinski, *German Army*, pp 33-34.

Emperor Napoleon I
Portrait by Jacques-Louis David, 1813

DER GENERALSTAB

[The Great General Staff] is the keystone of the whole system of German military organization... the cause of the great efficiency of the German army... acting as the powerful brain of the military body, to the designs of which brain the whole body is made to work.
- **British Major General Sir Henry Brackenbury, 1887**

In professional military circles, the development of the German General Staff is widely considered to be the greatest single achievement of the Prusso-German military tradition. Although outlawed twice during the 20th century, the General Staff achieved a prominence in Germany unequalled by any other military organization anywhere. Quite apart from its military utility, not since ancient Rome's Praetorian Guard has a military organization wielded so much political power and influence.

Copied as a model by almost every army in Europe, as well as Secretary Elihu Root's reform of the US Army in 1903, arguably no other military organization has been so controversial as the Prussian Great General Staff. Such military and political pre-eminence was not achieved overnight. The vaunted position of the German General Staff evolved over generations, during war and peace. In the decades preceding the Napoleonic Wars, the Prussian army had begun to evolve a staff system, not only to allow the control of ever-growing armies on the battlefield but, more importantly, to develop an over-arching system of national military authority. After Napoleon redefined warfare and shattered the once-proud Prussian army in 1806, the Prussian reformers remolded their military leadership and created a new and unique philosophy of military command and control.

The early work of the Prussian staff system was thereafter consolidated, restructured and refined. Only then did the newly created command and staff structure, guided by an elite group of commanders and staff officers, begin to bear fruit not just for Prussia but for Greater Germany.

The prodigious achievements of the Prussian staff system can only be understood by assessing the Prussian General Staff during the great span of its dominance in military affairs. From its embryonic beginnings up to the end of the 19th century. This chapter's focus will be upon the early development of the General Staff's functions within the army as well as the staff's subsequent rise to power as a political organ of the state. Just as important, however, will be the intellectual development that allowed and nurtured the growth of the leadership philosophy during this period of what would eventually come to be known as *Auftragstaktik*.

✠ ✠ ✠

It is a popular misconception that military staffs did not exist before the Napoleonic Wars. Indeed, there are records of the Egyptian, Roman, and other ancient armies having had staff officers to assist commanders control their armies. These assistants travelled with the commanders and acted as scribes or messengers. They were inevitably trusted senior men, usually noble-born themselves, who were charged to ensure the co-ordination of the various sub-components of the army. Normally the most important of these co-ordination problems was that of provisioning and quartering, thus the frequent appearance of the term 'quartermaster staff'. This is not to say that the commander had a staff *per se*. Initially, there was no special training required for someone to join the group surrounding the commander of an army. These assistants were selected either because they had political influence, or because they had some personal relationship with the commander. There was no recognizable structure. The commander of any force simply surrounded himself with as many people as he thought he needed. The number and type of assistants, or adjutants, grew proportionally with the size of the army, or the number of tasks that had to be performed.

Before beginning our investigation of the Prusso-German staff system, let us first establish the historical context within which our investigation will proceed. In the same way that modern British history is considered to begin with the Restoration of 1660, the creation of modern Germany is considered to begin with the Thirty Years War (1618-1648). This conflict over control of the Holy Roman Empire of the German Nation, a war that not only destroyed and depopulated most of Central Europe but also set practically all small German states against one another, brought to the fore the need for every state to have an effective army for, without one, no state could hope to survive. To use Thomas Hobbes' phrase, European life in the 17th century was 'nasty, brutish, and short.'

As we saw in the previous chapter, the struggle for political ascendency within the Holy Roman Empire was really a struggle between two extended families: the Catholic Hapsburgs and the Protestant Hohenzollerns. It is to the latter family that we now turn. Having produced a series of astute men to rule over the scattered possessions of the Margraviate of Brandenburg and acutely needing an effective army, there soon developed a special relationship between the Hohenzollerns and their armies. First established by the Great Elector, this special relationship, with the monarch as the unquestioned *Kriegsherr*, would remain unchallenged right up to the fall of the monarchy in 1918. Since the king was the first soldier of the state, the General Staff existed for only one reason: to assist him in the prosecution of his wars. Using this mandate as the basis for its existence, the General Staff evolved far beyond being merely a personal group of servants to the king. Using a term first coined by British writer Spencer Wilkinson in his 1890 book by the same name, he christened the German General Staff the 'brain of an army'. In the German case, it went beyond military effectiveness. The staff soon outgrew its specific military role to become a powerful political organ of the state.

One might naturally assume that any investigation of the Prussian General Staff begins with Frederick the Great. Generally regarded as the father of the German army, he introduced the formative changes and created the structures upon which much of the country's future successes were based. Frederick made the army the most proficient and, arguably, the most feared in Europe. Frederick's was the genius of tactical manoeuvre. He led his army as he led his country: single-handedly. Thus, historically, the roots of the Prusso-German General Staff system do not go back to Frederick, as has often been incorrectly assumed. He had no General Staff in any modern sense. Like military leaders before him, he had a cadre of officers who acted as aides, passed messages, and reconnoitred the battlefield for him. This group was the *Generalquartiermeisterstab* (General Quartermaster Staff), and Frederick acted as his own Chief of Staff. Through his own genius, ceaseless work, and iron discipline, Frederick was able to make this complex yet loose and uncoordinated system become an extension of his own personal will.

This complex system overwhelmed his two immediate successors. Frederick's weak and dissolute nephew, Frederick Wilhelm II, came to the throne upon his uncle's death in 1786. Unfortunately, he was unable to maintain the complicated machinery of state that his uncle had created and, almost immediately, Prussia began a slow decline. Like many large organizations in decline, those in power refused to admit the need for renewal. Prussia's military reputation remained strong, and neither the new king nor the army was inclined to reform a system that had proved so successful under the Great Frederick. The Prussian army had gained an aura of invincibility from Frederick's victories and his nephew was happy to leave that reputation untouched. The general belief that the army would be victorious if called upon remained prevalent not only within the army, but also within Prussia as a whole. Although Frederick Wilhelm II did manage to embroil Prussia in several conflicts, luckily for the hapless monarch, war with France amounted to little and the Second and Third Partitions of Poland, in 1793 and

1795, respectively, were little more than minor police actions. Though some might have recognized the beginnings of trouble, these actions were not any real test of the military structures or procedures. The view among the king, his ministers, and most of his officers remained that should the Corsican upstart in France attack Prussia, the army was more than a match for him.

The wars and campaigns of the French Revolution brought radical changes to European warfare and, though the Prussian army was not directly involved, by the 1790s there were calls for reform. Many officers wondered aloud, and in print, whether the new tactics and structures being practised by Napoleon should be adopted in the German states. Some officers, whose names would later become associated with the reform movement, were actively exchanging ideas and participating in open debate. There was no lack of opportunity to read about these new ideas. Military societies were plentiful, and correspondence and articles abounded. Among the most active of those openly calling for change and closely following the debates in professional journals was a Hanoverian army major, Gerhard Scharnhorst.

Gerhard David Johann Scharnhorst was born in a small village near Hanover on 12 November 1755. Son of a tenant farmer, he seemed destined to follow in his father's footsteps. But in 1772, the elder Scharnhorst inherited the Tegtmeyer estate, north-west of the city. The inheritance brought with it membership in the state *Landschaft*, the association of free landowners. This rise in status afforded the young Scharnhorst the opportunity for a formal education. The next year, Scharnhorst was enrolled as a cadet at Wilhelmstein, the academy of Frederick Wilhelm Ernst *Graf* zu Schaumburg-Lippe-Bückeburg "who for the next four years stimulated, guided, and cultivated Scharnhorst's character and intellect."[1] The *Graf* was a true son of the German *Aufklarung,* the German Enlightenment, and taught all his pupils that the mastery of the art of war required much more than parade drill and blind obedience. He taught his young cadets to broaden their minds in terms of culture, linguistics, and the humanities as well as the then accepted military subjects.[2]

In 1778, Scharnhorst reported to the Hanoverian 8th

Dragoons as a *Fähnrich,* or Ensign, and almost immediately was assigned lecturer duties in the regimental school at Nordheim. In 1782, Hanover established an artillery school, and the new commandant began looking for instructors; Scharnhorst's experience and intellect made him an obvious choice. He was a prolific writer, publishing an officer's handbook, a military field manual, as well as military studies on defence and on the reasons for the success of the French revolutionary armies. All these works gained Scharnhorst a well-deserved reputation for being a leading military theorist. However, he was without combat experience. In 1793, he left academe and reported for duty as a supernumerary battery commander during Hanover's involvement in the War of the First Coalition. He distinguished himself and foreshadowed the development of a command philosophy that would come to be associated with him. In September 1793, the English-Hanoverian army was in Belgium. The French attacked. "Sensing his moment, Scharnhorst, without orders, took command of several infantry units fleeing the battlefield, halted their rout, organized an effective rear-guard action, and conducted an orderly withdrawal that helped preserve the entire corps."[3] He went on to further impress and his actions eventually came to the attention of the Prussian king. He was offered a major's commission but declined. Scharnhorst did not want to face the same kind of frustration in the caste-ridden Prussian army as he had already suffered in Hanover. Instead, he negotiated a colonelcy as well as a brevet of nobility. It is an indication of Scharnhorst's reputation that Frederick Wilhelm III was willing to accept such terms, which he did.

Unlike today, in the 19th century, gentlemen frequently accepted commissions in foreign armies. It was both normal and respectable behaviour for army officers. Thus, in May 1801, Major Scharnhorst gave up his Hanoverian commission to become a lieutenant-colonel in the Prussian army. As promised for accepting the commission, the king ennobled him and made him a Count or *Graf.* He was posted to the *Generalquartiermeisterstab* in Berlin, and in July of that same year, joined the *Militärische Gesellschaft,* a social society of army officers lobbying for reform.

In fact, he was invited to be become a member and, at the first meeting he was elected by the membership to become the society's director. Officers who would later help change the Prussian army, mostly captains and lieutenants, flocked to the society. They included Lieutenant Carl von Clausewitz, Captain Wilhelm von Grolman, Lieutenant Rühle von Lilienstern, and Captain Hermann von Boyen. Clausewitz's reputation stands alone but the other three did not fade away; they all became Chiefs of the Prussian General Staff! "It is significant that these officers came ... not from the ranks of the rooted Pomeranian *Junkers* but from other regions and other sections of society."[4]

One of Scharnhorst's duties on the *Generalquartiermeisterstab* was to oversee military education. This charge made him the Director of Berlin's *Militärakademie*, with all the above officers as well as the Prussian crown prince, as his students. The Hanoverian's influence was quickly spreading. Although little progress in reforming the army was made by the time of Scharnhorst's arrival in Berlin, it would be unfair to say that Prussia had lain unchanged since the death of Frederick the Great. But change came slowly and in painfully small increments.

Soon after ascending to the throne in 1786, Frederick Wilhelm II, realizing that he needed help in running the army, had created a group of advisors to help him with his military affairs. Although Frederick the Great had held the reins of army leadership and administration wholly in his own hands, Frederick William II was overwhelmed by the task and created the *Oberkriegskollegium*, a central authority whose seven departments essentially dealt with the needs of the army's individual branches and schools:

> [It was] a committee formed of the heads of various agencies and boards dealing with such matters as supply, personnel, mobilization, veteran affairs, as well as with administration of the infantry, cavalry, artillery and engineers. Not all service bodies were represented. Such agencies as the General War Fund continued in charge of the civil bureaucracy; other organizations retained a more or less independent position – notably, the General Staff, at that time still in its infancy.[5]

The ever-reluctant king, continuing in the Prussian tradition of ministers reporting directly to him, did accept some suggestions for reform. The Third Partition of Poland in 1795 called for more forces than the army had, so the king created the *Immediat-Militär-Organisationskommission* to oversee the needed expansion, as well as to effect some minor reforms. The crown prince, soon to be Frederick Wilhelm III, became involved with the commission, which consisted of *Generalfeldmarschall* Heinrich von Möllendorff as president, and some officers drawn from the *Oberkriegskollegium*. The commission made several minor changes, mostly having to do with the employment of infantry. Despite this auspicious beginning, the reforms instituted by the *Kollegium* were superficial and did little to effect any real change in the Prussian army. The many different state organs, particularly those having to do with the military, continued in an uncoordinated effort to report directly to the king, just as had been the case for Frederick Wilhelm's uncle. Thus, when Frederick Wilhelm III ascended the throne in 1797, the army, having been kept out of the French Revolutionary Wars, was little changed from that of Frederick the Great:

> Except for a few minor changes the Prussian military institutions dating from the time of Frederick the Great remained much the same. It is almost unbelievable that a state which owed almost all of its fortune to the excellence of its army could watch with complacence the transformation of the French republican armies into a formidable military machine. This lethargy was almost entirely due to the timorous and procrastinating character of the monarchs.[6]

In Berlin's *Militärische Gesellschaft*, discussions were common suggesting exactly the type of reforms that the commission had begun. Some writers called for increased freedom of action at lower ranks, as well as the importance of the moral aspects of war – both ideas being fundamental to the future development of *Auftragstaktik*. Perhaps the two most distinguished and influential critics in Prussia in the period before Jena were Heinrich von Berenhorst and his pupil Heinrich von Bülow.

Both men called for more freedom for individual soldiers and argued for the acceptance of the importance of the moral and spiritual forces at work in warfare. They had a "profound influence on Clausewitz, and even the famous aphorism that war is merely the continuation of politics by other means is based on one of von Bülow's dicta."[7]

The early influence of the *Militärische Gesellschaft* as well as the concomitant intellectual intercourse upon the young Lieutenant von Clausewitz cannot be overstated. His inclusion among the reformers, where he became adjutant to Scharnhorst, would mark him for life. Later, this impact would manifest itself through Clausewitz's own teachings, first during his time as the director of the *Allgemeine Kriegsschule,* and then later when his seminal work, *On War,* became the touchstone not only of *Auftragstaktik,* but also of *Kriegskunst.*

In 1801, Colonel Christian Karl August Ludwig von Massenbach, an active member of the *Militärische Gesellschaft*, proposed a restructuring of the army. Originally having joined the Württemberg army in 1778, he accepted a Prussian commission from Frederick the Great in 1782 and was later decorated with a *Pour le Mérite.* His reform suggestions were wide-ranging, and some were quite extreme. He none-the-less became Chief of Staff to Prince Frederick Louis von Hohenlohe with unfortunate results at Jena. By 1803, General Levin von Geusau, the *Generalquartiermeister,* restructured the General Staff to establish three staff groups or 'brigades'. Each brigade was commanded by a lieutenant-colonel from the *Generalquartiermeisterstab.* These *Quartiermeisterleutnants* were subordinated directly to von Geusau himself. Eighteen staff officers, in the ranks of captain or major, supported them. The Commander of the Western Brigade was a recently recruited Hanoverian – von Scharnhorst. However, the restructured *Quartiermeisterstab* was too new to have any real effect on the army before it met Napoleon on the field at Jena.

After the Battle of Austerlitz in December 1805, it was becoming increasingly likely that the Prussians would soon have to meet the French in battle – despite a Franco-Prussian alliance signed in February 1806. Why this turnabout?

> One explanation for the change in Prussian policy lies in the personality of its monarch, Frederick Wilhelm III, who had come to the throne in 1797. Though a man of good intentions, he was characterized by weakness of will and vacillation, traits that are particularly unfortunate in an absolute ruler.[8]

Although the king had pursued a policy of neutrality, his wife, Louise von Mecklenburg-Strelitz, was not at all reluctant to voice her distaste for the French and soon became a driving force in the movement to confront Napoleon. So vocal was she that the queen was at one point dubbed 'the only man in Prussia'. By October 1806, Frederick Wilhelm III could vacillate no longer. The formation of the Confederation of the Rhine by Napoleon as a German dependency was irksome enough, but the possibility of Hanover being returned to the British moved Frederick Wilhelm III to conclude a secret treaty with Tsar Alexander I and to order the army to prepare for war. Pressure from the queen, intrigue by England, and the possibility of the loss of Hanover, finally forced him to act. Before the Russians could even ratify the treaty, the king sent an ultimatum to Napoleon to immediately withdraw all French troops from Germany. Napoleon was less than pleased at the Prussian king's impudence. He received the Prussian demand on 7 October and within days was marching towards Prussia. Before October had even ended, the French had shattered the Prussian army at Jena and were in Berlin dictating terms to the destroyed Prussians.

The Prussian army that moved to meet Napoleon in October 1806, was widely seen as the tactical heir of Frederick the Great and was reputed to be one of the finest in Europe:

> [This] Prussian Army – every bit as well-trained and well-drilled as Frederick's had been – was led to a humiliating defeat by Frederick Wilhelm III, in 1806, when he tried to teach some lessons to an upstart French ruler. That upstart happened to be Napoleon, and he destroyed Frederick Wilhelm's army in one brief day of battle on the fields of Jena and Auerstädt.[9]

Almost two centuries after the event, it is difficult to appreciate fully the watershed event that was the Battle of Jena. The battle and its aftermath are well-documented for it shocked Europe. For a modern equivalent, consider the reaction of the international community had the American-led Coalition been repulsed and destroyed in a single day during the invasion of Iraq in 1991! The loss was physical, moral, and political; it had a profound and long-lasting effect, reducing Prussia to approximately half its size, accepting French occupation and imposing a formidable war debt.

The opprobrious defeat at Jena was the catalyst needed to finally launch badly needed reforms. Frederick Wilhelm III had little choice but to order a complete investigation, as well as a ruthless restructuring of the army. As was the Prussian custom, the king appointed a new commission. He tasked the *Militärorganisationskommission* (Military Reform Commission) to investigate what had gone wrong at Jena. Convinced of cowardice among his officers, the king charged the commission to punish those who had been at fault, and to propose changes in organization, structure, training, and education. His choice of reformers was critically important and fateful. It would prove to change the course of Prussian military thinking for the next two centuries.

Although he could have no inkling of what was to happen, the king had set in motion the creation of a new school of warfare. The commission made many sweeping changes to the army, in effect rebuilding it from the ground up. Hundreds of officers were cashiered; thousands were retired. The brutal discipline imposed by Frederick the Great was removed; a form of universal service was introduced; the army was restructured; tactics were changed. The king's choice of officers for his commission was an interesting mix of reformers and conservatives. Following some internal squabbling and organizational bickering, the king wisely chose Scharnhorst to head the commission. Scharnhorst was most careful in how he set in motion the commission's work. He chose his young disciples, Boyen, Grolman, and his adjutant, Clausewitz, to be key players and it turned out to be auspicious for he would not live to see all their work brought to fruition. Most important among the reforms, however, were two structural changes attributable directly to Scharnhorst.

Thus, the Hanoverian Scharnhorst became the father of the Prussian General Staff. Structurally, he created two lasting organizations - the General Staff and the Ministry of War. By cabinet decree in 1808, the head of the *Generalquartiermeisterstab* was made head of the ministry, the king demurring to appoint a minister. This gave Scharnhorst nearly unfettered authority to institute change. This freedom of influence was short-lived, however. In 1809, due to pressure from the French, as well as from the conservative elements with the king's ear, Scharnhorst was removed as the head of the ministry. Nevertheless, as Chief of the General Staff, he continued to dominate the ministry and set about to give structure to the new department. He created a special section responsible for general military training and education of the army, as well as mobilization, intelligence, and the direction of tactics and strategy. "Scharnhorst retained the direction of this section and exercised a strong influence on the tactical and strategic thought of the officers in it by training them in war games and staff maneuvers."[10]

He intentionally kept the number of officers assigned to the General Staff small. There were only thirty-one in all. These officers were routinely posted to be adjutants to commanding generals across the army. This gave the Chief of the General Staff a heretofore unknown influence throughout the various brigades, divisions, and corps. It was Scharnhorst's intention that these men should alternate between field assignments and staff duty in Berlin, in order that they not lose touch with their tactical roots, much in the same way that modern armies like to alternate field command billets and staff billets to ensure a well-rounded experiential base for leaders. Scharnhorst developed this simple technique to ensure that military brilliance was not isolated or squandered. In effect, it was the selective seeding of General Staff officers throughout the army. Most if not all division, corps, and army headquarters had General Staff officers, either as their commanders, or more often, as the Chiefs of Staff. These officers were responsible not only to their field commanders, but also directly answerable to the Chief of the General Staff in the royal headquarters. The latter linkage being a separate, parallel, and independent chain of command.

The period of reform and rebuilding after the army's collapse at Jena changed the Prussian army forever. Scharnhorst and his followers had established the basis of a system unlike any in contemporary Europe. The General Staff not only gave assistance to the king and all senior commanders, but it also planned continuously for future possible wars. The old mold had been broken and a new one made. There was a critical difference between the staff system established by Scharnhorst and other systems extant in other armies at the time. The General Staff system was designed to change and to grow with the needs of the army. Since the staff was a self-regulating body, changes could be introduced based either upon the wants of the Chiefs of Staff, or by some external agency. By contrast, the system established by Frederick the Great was not at all flexible. He alone could make changes or improvements. As an extension of the king's personality, the staff had been at his mercy, and so in the case where a weak monarch sat on the throne, the army – and the nation – was in peril. Scharnhorst's new organization was specifically designed to remove that peril.

In June 1813, Scharnhorst unexpectedly died of a septic leg wound that he had received while campaigning against the French. His death was a serious blow to the reformers and their movement. But his years of fostering talent paid dividends and a deserving successor was found in his friend, General August Wilhelm Anton *Graf* von Gneisenau who, like Scharnhorst, was an import. Gneisenau had been born in Saxony in 1760 and was educated at Erfurt University. He served briefly in the Austrian cavalry before joining the Ansbach Regiment in 1782 and being sent to Canada as a mercenary for the British Crown. There are hints in several diaries that Gneisenau was first introduced to independent-thinking leaders while fighting against the French and Iroquois in Canada's forests. In 1786, he took a commission as a *Leutnant* in the Prussian army and served for the next two decades in almost complete obscurity. He came to prominence when he distinguished himself in the campaign of 1806-1807. Within several years, he went from being a forgotten captain to being a highly decorated and respected major-general. In 1811-1812 he travelled frequently between Austria, Russia, Sweden, and even England as the allies gathered to stem Napoleon's growing power.

Renewed hostilities in 1813 had found both Scharnhorst and Gneisenau on the staff of Field Marshal *Fürst* Gebhard von Blücher, who was then commanding the Silesian Army Corps. With Scharnhorst's death, Gneisenau was made Blücher's Chief of Staff. He not only continued the work of his predecessor but furthered it to the next stage. "He institutionalized the right of the commander's advisor to take part in command and control by advising the commander until he makes a decision."[11] The process soon proved its worth in the 1815 campaign against Napoleon, who had escaped Elba and once again taken France to war. With Gneisenau as Blücher's Chief of Staff, General Karl *Freiherr* von Müffling as the senior staff officer, and a series of hand-picked younger General Staff officers sprinkled throughout the rest of the army, the Prussians moved to assist the Allied commander, the Duke of Wellington, to meet the returned emperor. Although only in place for a few years, and already being eroded by a strong Prussian conservative backlash, the newly formed General Staff, which had already proven itself in the Wars of Liberation of 1813-14, would soon do so again. Founded by Scharnhorst and spread throughout the army by his disciples under Gneisenau's guidance, the new body of technically trained and intellectually freed officers laid the groundwork for the further development of *Auftragstaktik* and a new school of Prussian warfare. Officers chosen for the Staff embodied the qualities that Scharnhorst had valued most, those of intellect, military progress, patriotism, and nationalism.

Although nominally under the war ministry, after its initial decade of existence, the General Staff was poised for change. When Scharnhorst had re-organized the General Staff in 1809 he could not separate it from ministry control; but he had laid the foundations for an eventual split. This separation finally came in 1821. Frederick the Great's original construct, the *Generalquartiermeisterstab*, was officially renamed *Generalstab*. Blücher's erstwhile Chief of Staff von Müffling was now *Generalquartiermeister* and since he was senior to the Minister of War, General Rühle von Lilienstern, von Müffling was officially given the new title of Chief of the General Staff and made the highest military advisor by the King. However, the Chief of General Staff did not have the right of direct access, *Immediatvortrag*, to the king. He still had to seek an audience through the minister of war. A critical first step had been taken.

The formal split of the General Staff from the ministry was the first step making it a completely independent political organ of the state. The decision had far-reaching consequences for it enabled the General Staff to gradually take a leading hand in all military affairs. Finally separated from the political intrigues at the ministry, the Staff could now safeguard the leadership and command and control concepts initiated by Scharnhorst and matured by Gneisenau – those of *Auftragstaktik*. Further, the Staff could concentrate on improving the tactics and preparedness of the army – not merely after the outbreak of war, but also during peace and in preparation for war.

After the defeat of Napoleon, Europe in general, and Prussia in particular, suffered a predictable wave of conservative reaction. The post-war Congress of Vienna established a system to keep the peace but, in the process, stifled practically all reform across much of Europe. The period was a difficult one for the Prussian reformers. Gneisenau soon left active duty as his 1811 prediction came true: "Destiny will sweep us aside, the great and the small will once again behave in a miserable fashion ... the scoundrels who remain will rejoice and denigrate them."[12] By 1819, most of the reformers had either died, resigned or had been driven from the army. Nevertheless, the General Staff lived on.

The Prussian army, like all armies, needed to perform the functions of critical self-examination. Since 1786, the army had routinely formed special commissions entrusted to investigate problematic issues. The selected officers scrutinized specific problems, taking their findings directly to the king. In the 1820s, this function became officially embedded in the General Staff. As a mechanism to help ensure the continued maintenance of excellence, the specially trained and selected officers of the Staff would henceforth perform the routine of self-examination. Part of this scrutiny was the realization that sometimes not a strong enough link existed between theory and practice, or as Dupuy framed it:

> Knowledge and understanding of military theory and principles is not enough to assure truly effective battlefield performance; the ability to perform in accordance with theory must be so thoroughly ingrained in all leaders – and the soldiers too – that they will automatically perform their wartime tasks intelligently and flexibly.[13]

Recognizing the need to reinforce this linkage the Staff placed a continuing emphasis on translating theoretical problems into field maneuvers. These would act as the culmination of each year's training program, not only for the Staff, but for the entire army. The General Staff drew up the plans for these maneuvers. They were designed to take place in regions that might become theatres of war, and to emphasize responses to technical or tactical problems that seemed most currently significant to the branch inspectors.

Once established, these customs became ingrained in the Staff and survived through the decades up to the present day. Professor Williamson Murray, in a case study published in *Armed Forces and Society*, Winter 1981 "The German Response to Victory in Poland: A Case Study in Professionalism," details how the German General Staff did not rest on its laurels after the invasion of Poland in September 1939. Rather, the Staff studied the campaign in minute detail and ruthlessly restructured both the army and its training to better prepare for the upcoming invasion of France. The practice lives on. The senior class of the *FüAk* still writes tactical exercises for *Bundeswehr* field formations to implement.

In the four decades between the death of Scharnhorst and

Helmuth von Moltke's appointment as Chief of the General Staff, there were several important incidents within the Staff. Soon after the defeat of Napoleon, the principal embassies and each army corps had General Staff officers assigned to them. The Chief of Staff of each army corps was chosen from the General Staff. Initially seen by the corps commanders as spies from the royal headquarters in Berlin, these officers soon became the professional guiding hands to all the field commanders. Furthermore, since the immediate military superior of all these officers was not the corps commander but the *Chef der Großengeneralstabes* in Berlin, the Chief had a direct line of communication and influence in all corners of the army, both at home and abroad.

During the century known as the Concert of Europe (1815-1914), the reactionary movement within the army repeatedly clashed with the liberal reformers who were trying to bring broad-based democracy to Prussia. Although finally allowing non-noble officers, the officer corps had retained its aristocratic outlook and demeanour. The army had been used repeatedly to quell internal unrest; it was the army that had put down the revolts of 1848. The liberal movement had put great hope in the ascension to the throne of Frederick Wilhelm IV in 1840, but he proved to be a disappointment. Although making some progress with reforms, the army had continued to be isolated to the extent that in some cases the ideas of Scharnhorst had been stood on their head. "The Army was to be preserved, in the words of the director of the general war department, von Griesheim, as an island separated from society around it. Soldiers were not to be citizens in uniform, instead citizens were to become soldiers, a separate caste without the political rights of normal citizens."[14] It was a difficult period throughout Europe but particularly in Prussia and, at times, the internal stresses threatened to tear apart not only the army but the country as a whole.

If the army was to be an island in society, then the General Staff was to be even more isolated. From its origins as the font of reform, the General Staff soon moved in the opposite direction, becoming a focal point of anti-democratic militarism. "From its origins as a centre for reformers the General Staff developed itself into a reliable instrument of reactionary Prussian militarism. The politico-ideological foundation of its officers was starkly anti-democratic, conservative, and monarchical. The staff remained, however, free of feudal and absolutist trends."[15] Although disappointing from the standpoint of liberal democratic reform, this trend did not hamper the intellectual trends established by Scharnhorst and Gneisenau. The atmosphere in the Staff remained one of sober military production, with little or no concern for political involvement. Arguably, this potential flaw, the desire to avoid political involvement, could become a future liability in an organ of the state, but that dilemma lay in the future. As long as a strong monarch ran Prussia, there could be no conflict so far as the deeply loyal officers of the General Staff were concerned.

The year 1857 saw dramatic changes in Prussia. Amid economic crisis, Frederick Wilhelm IV's mental condition finally reached the point where he could no longer rule and his brother Wilhelm, the soldier-prince, was appointed as Prince Regent. Wilhelm had been an army officer all his adult life and was a veteran of the Napoleonic Wars. He noticed in his son's tutor and aide-de-camp Helmuth von Moltke, a particularly bright officer: "This extraordinary soldier had made his way up through the peacetime Prussian army. That he remained a second lieutenant for twelve years reflected no lack of confidence in him, for his superiors had sent him through the three-year war school and appointed him to the general staff."[16] Von Moltke had gone on to serve as a General Staff officer with the Turkish Pasha, and by the time he came to the attention of the prince regent was one of the most well-educated and experienced staff officers in the army. One of Wilhelm's first acts as the regent was to make von Moltke the acting Chief of the General Staff.

Helmuth Karl Bernhard *Graf* von Moltke was born in Mecklenburg in 1800, and as a youth served in the Danish army. In 1821, he applied for and was granted a subaltern's commission in the Prussian *Leibgrenadier* Regiment. He was a highly intellectual individual with a passion for languages and reading. He translated, for instance, Gibbon's *Decline and Fall of the Roman Empire* as well as multiple novels from English to German. During his seventy years in the Prussian army, he would come to epitomize the embodiment of the gentlemanly, literate, and learned Prussian General Staff officer.

Although fortuitous, the appearance of von Moltke was not completely unexpected. Although no one could have foreseen the arrival of someone as brilliant and professional as he, the creation by Scharnhorst and Gneisenau of the educational and training system and its embodiment as the General Staff ensured that men of aptitude and quality would eventually come to the fore. It was precisely the inability to count upon the appearance of genius that made the concept of a General Staff so valuable. By design, almost any officer who had risen through the ranks of the General Staff to become its Chief could be counted upon to be professionally competent. Thus, "Scharnhorst's objective had been achieved. The collective brain of the General Staff had brought institutionalized military excellence to Prussia."[17]

The rise of Prussia, of its army, and the concomitant rise of Prussian militarism are all bound together with the brilliance of Moltke. Early in his tenure, he set about to stamp his own personality on the General Staff by reorganizing it. In fact, von Moltke reorganized the General Staff at least twice. The first time was immediately after he became the Chief; the second was after the Austrian war. Military history, rather than being the responsibility of one of the staff departments, was made a central concern for the Staff institutionally and for its officers as individuals. "Moltke believed that strategy could benefit greatly from history, provided it was studied with the right sense of perspective."[18] His experience as advisor to the Turkish Pasha as well as his observations of Giuseppe Garibaldi's campaign to unify Italy, convinced him that a reasonable plan well executed was preferable to a good plan poorly employed. Moltke drew heavily from the teachings of Scharnhorst and Clausewitz, as well as Gneisenau's critical concept of *Führen durch Auftrag*. He took great pains to expand upon these concepts and push them throughout the army. "Much in contrast to the vaunted Prussian discipline, a premium was placed upon independent judgement of all officers."[19]

Although untested in war, the General Staff was a successfully functioning organ when Moltke was placed at its head. Under his tutelage he would make it the envy of practically every army in the world. Not long after the startling victories over Denmark in 1864, Austria in 1868, and France in 1870, all major armies around the world moved to establish some form of General Staff based on the Prussian model; but not all armies did so successfully:

> In the French, Austrian, and British armies, staff officers, submerged beneath their weight, became little more than military bureaucrats, out of touch with and despised by their regimental colleagues. Moltke, on the contrary, turned them into an élite, drawn from the most promising regimental officers, trained under his eye and alternating in their careers between staff and command posts of increasing responsibility.[20]

In addition to intellectual development, Moltke continued the practice of annual staff rides in critical frontier areas each year to give the staff officers extra experience and practice in dealing with unexpected problems (which he would throw at them without warning). The years of turmoil and development begun by the early reformers were beginning to pay dividends. Scharnhorst's structure, which was then refined by Gneisenau and the intervening Chiefs of Staff, began to bear fruit under Moltke's masterful direction. The General Staff had demonstrated not only an institutionalization of excellence, arguably even genius, it had also demonstrated an ability to methodically produce and reproduce this excellence. This was a trait which, up to that point, was unique to the Prussian General Staff.

After Scharnhorst's foundational work in separating the General Staff from the ministry of war in his reorganization of 1809, it was but a matter of time for the separation to become real. After 1821 there had been, in effect, a triad of forces that affected Hohenzollern military policy. This triad was composed of the war ministry, the military cabinet, and the General Staff.

Until the rise of Moltke, General Albert von Roon was minister of war. Roon was not only Wilhelm I's most trusted military advisor during this politically tumultuous era, but he was also the most influential figure in the army before the Austrian War. Having already shown an inkling of his tactical acumen in the victory over Denmark in 1864, Moltke came into his own during the Austrian War. To show his appreciation, Wilhelm elevated the status of the Chief of the General Staff. Up to that point, the Chief of Staff had been responsible only for planning, but now the king allowed Moltke, in time of war, to issue operational orders on his behalf. He did not need to seek permission from the war ministry. He needed only *inform* the ministry.

This indulgence from the king effectively emancipated the General Staff from the political forces within his government. Moltke kept adding to his record of victories. A similarly impressive performance against the Austrians in 1866, where he was held to be singlehandedly responsible for the almost complete envelopment of the Austrians at Königgrätz, delighted the king. This victory finally gave Prussia the upper hand in the centuries-long struggle between the ruling houses of Hohenzollern and Hapsburg. A short four years later, Moltke repeated his successes, this time against the reputedly most powerful military in Europe. Prussia's rapid defeat of Napoleon III's armies completed the *de facto* emancipation of the Staff. All that was needed was to have it embedded in law. It did not come immediately, but it did come. With the Kaiser's blessing, a cabinet order on 24 May 1883, placed the Chief of the General Staff on par with both the war ministry and the military cabinet.[21] The General Staff was now separated not only *de facto* but also *de jure* from the ministry of war.

The Austro-Prussian War highlighted both the leadership techniques that Moltke had been stressing and the problems in the Staff that needed correction. However strong Moltke's reputation was before 1866, the war with Austria confirmed that his genius would outlive him. During the short seven weeks of conflict, the Chief of General Staff employed all the techniques that had been developed since the reforms of 1806. Foremost, he embodied the spirit of *Auftragstaktik*. Moltke gave the Army Corps Commanders guidance – not detailed orders – and even the guidance was only what was essential. He refused to become too involved in the lower-level tactical engagements and held himself back from interfering when his plans did not unfold exactly as he had planned. He employed the intelligence section of the General Staff to great effect, using them to decide where to send the various army corps. The system of sprinkling General Staff officers throughout the army and making all the Chiefs of Staff responsible to him at the royal headquarters was used to maximum effect. Through these men Moltke tracked not only the movements of the senior commanders but far more importantly, he tracked their *intentions*. Gneisenau's *Führen durch Auftrag* had come to full maturity.

After the war, as was the well-established procedure after any major operation or exercise, Moltke ordered the war studied, the lessons drawn from this study and then fully implemented. Although flush with victory, the General Staff saw room for improvement. Part of their cultural ethos dictated that there was always room for improvement. The Staff was again restructured to make it more efficient. The last of Moltke's great victories, the Franco-Prussian War of 1870-71, was in many ways a replay of the previous war. Moltke, along with Bismarck, was lionized and seen as having been instrumental in the founding of the new Germany. In 1888, Wilhelm II took the crown of Greater Germany as *Kaiser* Wilhelm I and General Karl *Graf* von Waldersee succeeded Moltke as Chief of the General Staff. Although the Great War was still unforeseeable, storm clouds were beginning already to gather on the horizon of German politics. The petulant new emperor did not see his Chancellor's political maneuvering in a positive light. They quarrelled and in 1890, Bismarck, in many respects the founder of the German Empire, was forced into retirement. Waldersee did not last long either. His disagreements with the *Kaiser* caused Wilhelm to remove him in 1891.

Politics, policy, and statecraft were not part of the Staff's remit and as Wilhelm's imperial ambitions grew (his quest for 'a place in the sun') so did the military's ability to quench his thirst for martial glory. The Franco-Prussian War, a shocking upset to most who were paying attention, was the great crucible that had finally brought, in Dupuy's words, the concept of institutionalized excellence to full fruit. Almost a century later, in his seminal book *The Decisive Battles of* the *Western World,* General JFC Fuller's judgement was that France's defeat at the hands of the Prussians lay not in military strength or in armaments. The decisive factor was the relative strengths of the two General Staffs. Napoleon's genius had acted as a brake on the development of a professional staff system. He had always used a *personal* staff. The French did not recognize this failing. Thus, when the Prussians and French again met in battle in 1870, the French general staff of the *Deuxième Empire* was, in Fuller's phrase, a collection of 'popinjays' and 'greybeards' and were not trusted by the army commander, who forbade them to even appear in the field! The results are well known.

✠ ✠ ✠

Thus, with the ascent of Moltke to the office of Chief of the General Staff, the reforms of Frederick the Great's group of advisors had come fully of age. As a separate and specially trained branch of the army, the General Staff led the Prussian army out of the dark days after Jena. Perhaps more importantly, the defeat at Jena had been the catalyst needed to fuse together two independently progressing trends: the continued feudal link between the officer corps and the Prussian crown; and the development of a professional General Staff system enabling the institution of the army to serve as a vital organ of state policy, irrespective of how strong, or weak, the head of state might be. The result of this union was the creation of the guiding structure of the *Großengeneralstab*. In turn, what this structure precipitated was the intellectual rebirth of the Prussian army.

NOTES

[1] Charles Edward White, *The Enlightened Soldier, Scharnhorst and the Militärische Gesellschaft in Berlin, 1801-1805*, (Westport CT, 1989), p. 3.

[2] *Ibid*, pp. 5-6.

[3] *Ibid*, p.16.

[4] Walter Görlitz, *History of the German General Staff 1657-1945*. Translated by Brian Battershaw, (New York, 1961), p 19.

[5] Peter Paret, "Yorck and the Era of Prussian Reform 1807-1815" in *Makers of Modern Strategy: from Machiavelli to the Nuclear Age*, Peter Paret, ed. (Princeton, 1966), p.99.

[6] Walter O. Shanahan, *Prussian Military Reforms 1786 –1813*, (New York, 1945), pp.68-69.

[7] Martin Kitchen, *A Military History of Germany, A Military History of Germany from the eighteenth century to the present day*, (London, 1975), p. 33

[8] Charles Breunig, *The Age of Revolution and Reaction 1789 – 1850*, (New York, 1970), pp.87-88.

[9] T. N. Dupuy, *A Genius for War: The German Army and General Staff, 1807 – 1945*, (Englewood Cliffs NJ, 1977), p.9.

[10] Hajo Holborn, "The Prusso-German School: Moltke and the Rise of the General Staff" in *Makers of Modern Strategy: from Machiavelli to The Nuclear Age*, Peter Paret, ed., (Princeton NJ, 1986), p. 282.

[11] Christian Millotat, *Understanding the Prussian-German General Staff System*, (Carlisle Barracks, PA, 1992), p. 30.

[12] Kitchen, p. 60.

[13] Dupuy, *Genius for War*, p. 67.

[14] Kitchen, p.95.

[15] Helmut Otto, *Schlieffen und der Generalstab* (Berlin, 1966), p. 15.

[16] Jones, *Art of War*, p.397.

[17] Dupuy, p.44.

[18] Holborn, "The Prusso-German School" p. 290.

[19] *Ibid*, p. 291.

[20] Howard, European History, pp. 100-101. The alternation of regimental and General Staff duty was not a Moltkean innovation. Scharnhorst had instituted the idea so that young officers did not lose touch with their troops. It had lapsed after his death.

[21] Millotat, p. 35.

Feldmarshal Fürst Gebhard von Blücher

Oil on copper by Peter Edward Stroehling c. 1826

FÜHREN DURCH AUFTRAG

If I wrote the prescription, he [Gneisenau] made the pills!
- **Feldmarshal Fürst Gebhard von Blücher**

he French Revolution of 1789 had introduced dramatic changes to the linear warfare of the 18th century. The rigid, disciplined professional armies, as epitomized by Frederick the Great's Guards regiments, although still very much the backbone of European armies, were being badly mauled by light infantry and skirmishers. The use of these irregular skirmishers, so-called *tirailleurs,* called for independent thinking, new tactics, and better training. More importantly, they called for a shift in how leaders at all levels perceived battle—and how they led troops in battle. Slow, precise, geometric formations, which required formed troops that were highly drilled and brutally disciplined, were coming up against the hit and run tactics of small skirmishing groups, who hit without warning and then melted away. Light infantry skirmishers were being trained to think for themselves and to use ground cover to best effect. Mindless drill, where soldiers walked into walls of lead shot, was slowly being forced to give way to flexibility of both thought and action by more highly trained individuals.

These battlefield developments were being discussed in the military literature of the era, but no significant alteration in how armies fought appeared until the French shattered their ancient monarchical system and put a nation of peasants into uniform. The new tactics and massive armies of the French *levées en masse,*

combined with the opening of officers' commissions to non-aristocrats, resulted in a dramatic alteration in land warfare. The result was a synergistic effect. Tactics, structures, and leadership all evolved in concert with each other to sweep away the outdated methods of fighting.

Armies are living organizations. They require nurturing and training. Someone must create ideas which become embedded as doctrinal principles and then go on to become part of the army's routine. The Roman legions did not one day suddenly decide that they should dig fortifications whenever they stopped for the night. The concept came from Roman tactical doctrine that had been learned in battle from the Greeks, developed, tried, and tested. Likewise with the Prussians after Jena. Something had gone terribly wrong, and Prussia had paid a heavy price. The army had been confident of its skills and its doctrine, and it had nonetheless been roundly defeated. To avoid paying such a price again, Scharnhorst and his reformers not only altered the army's structure, but they also adopted new and sometimes radical ideas that grew to become part of the army's culture. Of all these ideas, the most successful was the concept of *Auftragstaktik*, that a commander could trust a subordinate to do what was best – even without orders.

It is not possible to fully appreciate *Auftragstaktik* without understanding the trends in Prusso-German thinking that created this leadership philosophy. This chapter investigates those trends. Beginning with the transformation of battle and tactics heralded by the French Revolution and consequent Napoleonic Wars, the major milestones in Prussian, and then German, military history will be examined. The creation and development of the General Staff is intimately intertwined with the foundation and evolution of *Auftragstaktik*. It is impossible to disentangle the two; one could not have been cultivated without the other. Although the development of the General Staff has already been discussed at some length, for clarity it, occasionally, will be briefly revisited.

✠ ✠ ✠

It was not long after the death of Frederick the Great in 1786 that the political map of Europe began to change. As previously discussed, his nephew Frederick Wilhelm II, not as militarily gifted as his famous uncle, did little to affect the army that he had inherited. Frederick's nephew died in 1797, and his son Frederick Wilhelm III inherited his grandfather's highly complex governmental structure along with his father's reticence to use the army. Consequently, Frederick Wilhelm III was slow to act against the French. For this reason, Prussia was the last of the European powers to attempt to stem the rise of Napoleon.

The Prussian army was all but destroyed by Napoleon at the twin battles of Jena and Auerstädt. With the Prussian military in ruins and the myth of invincibility revealed, Prussia was suddenly in grave danger. The term used in German literature, then and now, for the 1806 defeat was *der Zusammenbruch Preußens* – the collapse of Prussia. This loss at Jena was not seen solely as a *military* failure. Jena was a *national* catastrophe. Slow to move before, Frederick Wilhelm III now had no choice. Of dire necessity, the Prussian army had to re-create itself, and the obvious model stood before them. Napoleon had swept away the Bourbon French army and had created the most modern army of the age. He had wrought a fundamental change in how wars were henceforth to be fought. It was not that there was a reluctance to adopt the French forms of war, for the outward forms were easily taken on, and there was certainly no lack of interpreters of Napoleon's genius. From contemporaries to subordinates to adversaries, men such as Jomini and Clausewitz had discerned deep insights into the keys to French successes. However, almost everyone focused upon the physical manifestations of Napoleon's battle tactics. They ascribed Napoleon's success to what we, in modern terms, would call 'battlespace dominance'. This dominance led to what author Douglas A. MacGregor, in *Breaking the Phalanx*, has described as a strategic focus within which Napoleon planned a series of sequential operations and engagements. The culminating action would come in a dominating maneuver, whose purpose was to destroy the enemy's army. That was true, but that was not all.

Fortunately for Prussia, there was a small group of officers who saw not only the need for radical change, but also saw that Napoleon's victories came from more than just innovative tactics. These officers, mostly concentrated in the Berlin *Militärische Gesellschaft,* saw beyond the obvious mimicry of adopting French formations and tactics. They saw the need for an original interpretation of what Napoleon had achieved. Through deep analysis and discussion, they were able to capture the essence of Napoleonic warfare. In turn, they distilled this original interpretation into an institutional manifestation of battlefield leadership that would grow to become the very heart of *Auftragstaktik.* This distillation would shortly come to be called *Absicht des [Obergeordneten] Führers* or what has come to be known in English as [Superior] Commander's Intent – to this day, a key component of doctrine throughout NATO without which *Auftragstaktik* would not be possible.

The Prussian army's first encounter with Napoleon forced a transformation that was at once radical and fundamental. In effect, the army was destroyed and reborn. To understand this rebirth, we must understand that the Prussian army of the 19th century was really the creation of four very different men, two by legacy and two by design. These men were Frederick the Great, Napoleon, Scharnhorst and Gneisenau.[1] The work of Frederick had been elemental. He had not only given the army its structure, but he had also embodied, in his own persona, the army's mind and spirit. As well as establishing the regimental traditions and iron discipline necessary to be victorious in the 18th century, he had given the army its soul. By making himself the first soldier of the state, he had lent his personality to the army; he had given it its *Korpsgeist.* But Frederick, like so many brilliant leaders before and since, had not established an organization that would operate without him. In blindly maintaining the traditions of Frederick, the Prussian army after him had not grasped the significance of Napoleon's revolution in military affairs. Ironically, two non-Prussian officers, Scharnhorst and Gneisenau, had. Along with the other reformers, they now had to force the army to rebuild itself. To do so, they needed a new paradigm. Only in this way might the army, once again, enjoy the battlefield pre-eminence that it had under Frederick II:

> The catastrophe of Jena in 1806 vindicated most signally the ideas of these men – Gerhard von Scharnhorst, Hermann von Boyen, August von Gneisenau, Carl von Clausewitz. Scharnhorst, their leader, was appointed President of the Military Reorganization Commission set up after Jena to remodel the Prussian Army. It was clearly not enough mechanically to imitate such French formations and techniques as the divisional system and the employment of light infantry.[2]

Prussia's precarious geo-political situation necessitated an army that could be used as a reliable instrument of state policy. The collapse at Jena and Auerstädt, was far more than a humiliation. It brought into question the continued use of the army to execute state policy. "If the Army was to remain 'a sharp, reliable weapon' in the hands of its kings" then only two practical possibilities for national survival existed.[3] Either the state had to reverse one hundred and fifty years of history and move to a diplomatic alternative to satisfy the needs of national security, or it needed to find a way to ensure that the army could once again be made the enduring and reliable underpinning of the state. In the turbulent political atmosphere of early 19th century Europe, this was Hobson's choice. In convening the *Militärorganisationskommission* Frederick Wilhelm III set into motion wide-ranging reforms that would change not only the internal workings of his army, but they would also reset the philosophical underpinnings of how the Prussians henceforth viewed war.

The king appointed Scharnhorst as president of the commission which, initially at least, included not only supporters but also opponents of reform. Scharnhorst removed the opponents. He set a series of questions for the commission to consider including how the army was to perform in battle and how it was to be organized, armed, and employed. Scharnhorst's first step was to review the selection and training of officers. King's commissions were made more available to men not of noble birth, and promotion was henceforth to be based on merit:

> These new times call for more than title and pedigree; they call for action and strength. This the monarch has considered, because he has given equal access to the talents of all within the realm for military promotion and employment. He has removed all encumbrances to those previously barred by law simply because of their lineage or because of nepotism.[4]

The introduction of the bourgeoisie into the officer ranks was met with a reaction that bordered on horror. Most officers of the old school saw it as an attack, not only upon their status as officers, but upon their whole social class.[5] The fact that Scharnhorst was not even Prussian and had only received a patent of nobility in 1801 only made the reaction worse. Not surprisingly, the reformers were not widely supported in their attempts to change the army. In particular, the *Junker* class, which for generations had maintained a virtual monopoly on officership, was reluctant to change *their* army, one that many *Junkers* felt had been the model for all others to emulate. In 1803, well before encountering Napoleon in battle, the widespread response to the 1795 *Immediat-Militär-Organisationskommission* had been that it was ridiculous to expect that an army as successful and expert as Prussia's "which for so long was held to be the unattainable model for all Europe, could undertake a complete change to its constitution and its being, and thereby reduce itself to the level of a local Militia."[6]

Despite warnings, the army had continued to believe steadfastly in its own infallibility, with results that have been discussed. The post-1806 reforms had set the Prussian army on the road to revitalization and, even more important than offering officers' commissions to worthy young men, had restructured the army's education system. Although his *Militärakademie* was dissolved after Jena, as head of the Reform Commission, Scharnhorst founded the *Allgemeine Kriegsschule,* the General War College in Berlin in 1809, which would later evolve into the famous *Kriegsakademie.* Frederick the Great had made his army the school of the state. Now it was up to the reformers to rebuild that school so that it might safeguard the state.

The sad truth was that education in Prussia had fallen behind its neighbours. Thus, it was not just army officers that needed better education. Both the civilian and military education systems needed rebuilding. In line with the social reforms begun by Baron Heinrich vom und zum Stein, many of the class restrictions within Prussian society began to be loosened. Stein was also a leading member of the king's Reform Commission, but his interests were focused primarily upon the social and political aspects of reform rather than on the purely military initiatives. Meanwhile, Prussian Minister of Education Wilhelm von Humboldt set about reforming education for the nation. Humboldt was the father of humanistic education in Germany. In 1809, he founded the University of Berlin and opened secondary education to a much broader spectrum of the population. What Humboldt was doing for the state, Scharnhorst set about doing for the army.

There is a substantial collection of literature that focuses upon the work of the reformers and their commission. Unfortunately, the emphasis of most of this study has invariably been on the physical or the structural changes that they made. To be sure, much was done in this respect. *Jäger* battalions, with their *tirailleur* tactics, and their *primus inter pares* leadership, were successfully introduced. There was real if limited success in the introduction of national conscription and the creation of a *Landsturm*, or peoples' national defence force. The *Krümper*, or national reserve system, was built and, the most lasting achievement of all, the *Landwehr* or Reserve Army was created, which lasted practically unchanged until the demise of the monarchy. All these changes were of great significance. They brought new tactics, fresh ideas, and foreign influences into the staid and intellectually stiff Prussian army. More importantly, these changes all allowed the nation to identify with its army more closely. The existence of bourgeois officers tended to break down some of the feudal barriers that had been in place for generations. Despite *Junker* resistance to all these changes, once the barriers started to come down, it proved impossible to erect them again.

More important than all the structural changes were the changes in leadership philosophy. Too often overlooked by historians, the critical element among the Prussian reforms was the intellectual shift that had been forced to occur. Even before the reformers were given their charge by the king, Scharnhorst's society of young officers had paid close attention to the new and evolving French tactics. Scharnhorst's *Militärische Gesellschaft* had become an intellectual breeding ground not only for the reform movement but also for new ideas that would later become embedded in Prussian tactical doctrine. Among the many philosophical changes after 1806, no single development became as important as the concept of carrying out the will of a superior commander – with or without direct orders. This concept of *Führen durch Auftrag* [Leading by Mission] would come to be known as *Auftragstaktik*. Various translations into English as 'Mission Command' or 'Mission Style Orders' do not capture the sense. The real issue was not technical – it was conceptual. Commanders told subordinates what they were to accomplish; subordinates then decided how the commander's will was to be translated into action. Even before the Battle of Waterloo, the Prussian General Staff began inculcating everyone: first the bright new leaders and then, through them, the rest of the army. No other single aspect of the Prussian way of war would play as powerful a role as this deceptively simple idea:

> In the revitalized General War School in the years between 1809 and 1813, and again in 1814, Scharnhorst first, and later Gneisenau, Boyen, and Grolman, had demanded that the lessons of the 1806 and 1807 campaigns be studied intensively. Particularly emphasized in these classes, and in occasional seminars of high-level commanders, was the fact that French victories of 1806 and 1807 were won by the complete and aggressive responsiveness of French commanders to the will of Napoleon, even without specific directives from the Emperor and even when they were miles away from his direct supervision. This had not only been significant in the French victories at Jena-Auerstädt and Friedland but had been even more important in the relentlessness and effectiveness of the French pursuit after these battles. If there was any single historical example which

Scharnhorst and Gneisenau cited more than any other in trying to indoctrinate the new leadership of the Prussian Army, it was that of the French pursuit from Jena to the Baltic Sea in 1806. [7]

Even a cursory study of the Napoleonic Wars makes evident that Napoleon was most successful when his marshals fully understood his intent. As an admirer of Frederick the Great, Napoleon kept all the controls for battle firmly in his own hands. Although he had a Chief of Staff, Marshal Berthier, as well as a plethora of staff officers to carry out his instructions, Napoleon, like Frederick, essentially did all his own planning; "Berthier was never more than the great man's chief clerk."[8] Most importantly, Napoleon kept his own counsel. Unlike Blücher's relationship with Scharnhorst, and later with Gneisenau, Napoleon did not share command with anyone. He did, however, explain his intent to his marshals and corps commanders. When his intent was understood and executed – *Auftragstaktik* – success was usually the result.

Admittedly, the central importance of *Auftragstaktik* has not been universally accepted. Citing historians like Michael Howard and Herbert Rosinski, the widely accepted argument has been that Scharnhorst's most significant contribution was his introduction of universal conscription and the consequent rise in Prussian nationalism. They argue that national conscription was the single most important change made by the Prussian army, and therefore the foundation of its reborn effectiveness. But that is, in my opinion, short sighted. Though true that this structural change in how the army recruited and trained soldiers had a great impact, it is also true that conscription was an important factor, the value of which I do not dispute. In line with Napoleon's axiom that the moral is to the physical as three is to one, I believe that the evidence points elsewhere. I remain convinced that save for his creation of the General Staff, Scharnhorst's, and thereafter Gneisenau's, single greatest contribution was the intellectual shift away from Frederician tight control of battlefield manoeuvre, the relaxing of the taut reins of command, and the inculcation up and down the chain of command of the idea that commanders were to trust their subordinates and make them, in Professor McAndrew's words, 'shareholders of operations' and not just 'un-consulted employees.'

Historian Gerhard Ritter's comment that the most important change needed was to replace the soulless, professional army with a whole nation in arms was true, but it did not go far enough in explaining Prussian success. The Prussians did adopt French formations and structures, but the adoption of the French notion of a nation in arms came relatively late, and only in modified form. In any case, although conscription may have given the Prussian army greatly increased manpower, and thereby changed the physical structure of the army, this argument misses the point. It was the conceptual uniqueness of *Führen durch Auftrag* [*Auftragstaktik*], or *Absicht des Führers* [Commander's Intent], that made the Prussians different from all their contemporaries. No other army, up until the end of this century adopted the principle of acting in accordance with the spirit of orders – even to the point of disobedience. There were other influences to be sure, but even if it were forced to stand alone, one could easily credit *Auftragstaktik* with being the single most important characteristic of Prusso-German *Kriegskunst*. Certainly, no intellectual change could have survived without some of the more fundamental organizational and social reforms. But that misses the point. If one imagines what might have occurred had the intellectual seeds not been planted in, and by, the minds of men like Scharnhorst, Gneisenau, Grolman, Boyen, and Clausewitz, one might predict that the Prussian army would have become somewhat better. The simple use of the French notion of divisions and army corps and the doctrine of *Gefecht der verbündeten Waffen*,[9] or Combined Arms Theory, with its subsequent near-evangelical application, would certainly have gone a long way to improve the battlefield proficiency of the Prussian army. What it would not have done, however, was to have re-invented Prussian warfare.

By 1810, all the old basic schools, except the two cadet schools, *die Kadetenhaüser;* in Berlin and Potsdam, had been dissolved. In their places, new schools of war were established in Berlin, Königsberg, and Breslau, offering nine-month courses to give candidates for commissions broader educational foundations to better prepare them to become army officers. For the general 'spiritual advancement' of officers, a superior military academy was founded in Berlin. This was *Die Allgemeine Kriegsschule*, the General War College, which would later become the famous *Kriegsakademie*. There, small groups of selected officers were given a three-year course in military specialities: mathematics, tactics, strategy, artillery, military geography, French, German, physics, chemistry, equitation, and military administration. From these new beginnings would come the graduates who would go on to crystallize the concepts of warfare that would create the Prussian school of war. The *Kriegsakademie* would come to play a crucial role. "The upper class of this academy, the so-called *Selekta*, became the chief recruiting ground for the General Staff..."[10] In effect, the new Prussian education system would become a life support system for Scharnhorst's newly created General Staff.

Another intellectual shift unique to the Prussian school occurred in the interim between Jena and ultimate victory at Waterloo. In 1812, Scharnhorst was appointed as Chief of Staff to the seventy-year-old Field Marshal Blücher, whom he had first met late in 1806, just before the two of them were taken prisoner near Lübeck. The old Hussar, a "rough, and thoroughly ill-educated man"[11] had an immense respect for his intelligent and well-trained Chief of Staff and considered him to be much more than merely his *Stabschef*. Above and beyond the mundane duties of Chief of Staff, Scharnhorst became Blücher's *Führergehilfe* on command, control, and tactics.[12]

The unique relationship that developed between these two men is considered today, by the *Bundeswehr*, to be the foundation of the concept of shared responsibility between a commander and his chief of staff and it forms one of the fundamental pillars of *Auftragstaktik*.[13]

After Scharnhorst's untimely death in 1813, his fellow reformer Gneisenau took his place both as Chief of the General Staff and as Blücher's Chief of Staff. Although a completely different personality from his friend and mentor, he shared many of Scharnhorst's ideas. To an even greater degree than Scharnhorst, Gneisenau's association with Blücher highlighted the uniquely Prussian concept of shared responsibility between a commander and his Chief of General Staff and has been described as arguably the ultimate association between commander and subordinate in the history of military command. In the preparatory battles before Waterloo (Quatre Bras and Ligny, 16 June 1815), the Field Marshal was seriously injured when his horse fell on him. Gneisenau assumed command and made the fateful decision to withdraw the corps to the village of Wavre. The Field Marshal had been feared dead but once he was found, a dispute erupted between him and Gneisenau. The old gentleman had given his word to Wellington that he would support the British position, but Gneisenau harboured a deep distrust of the British and did not want to rush to Wellington's aid. Blücher, although unwell, was still in titular command. Arguably, it should have been a simple matter of issuing the order to move the army, but for Blücher it was not. He felt deeply that he needed the Gneisenau's concurrence since he was the Chief of Staff. After the battle, Blücher remarked that the reason they moved on to Waterloo was because Gneisenau had finally 'given in' to him. One cannot imagine such an argument arising between Wellington or Napoleon and *any* of their subordinates.

The implications of such shared responsibility within the chain of command were both obvious and revolutionary. The Chief of the General Staff shared responsibility for the mission with his commander. This fundamental tenet of *Auftragstaktik*, not found in any other army, stemmed at least partially from the dual responsibility that Gneisenau had both as the Chief of the General Staff and as the Chief of Staff to Blücher. This idea of shared responsibility soon became institutionalized and evolved as an unwritten custom that gave Chiefs of General Staffs the right to enter dissenting opinions in their war diaries, a practice that would remain in effect until the 20th century. Before his own untimely death due to cholera in 1831, Gneisenau along with his own Chief of General Staff, Carl von Clausewitz, made at least one other enduring change to Prussian warfare. He instituted a habit that would allow him to rightly be called the father of *Auftragstaktik*:

> He was the first to develop command and control
> by directives, thus giving latitude to the subordinate

commanders ... [who] were for the first time issued directives expressing the intent of the Royal headquarters in terms of clear objectives but giving only general indications of the methods of their achievement. This enabled commanders and their General Staff officers to use initiative in taking advantage of unforeseen opportunities, provided that their actions were consistent with the main objective. Thus, Gneisenau laid the cornerstone of the German leadership philosophy: mission-oriented command and control.[14]

Clearly, if anyone can be credited as giving birth and impetus to *Auftragstaktik*, it must be Gneisenau. Although not nearly as well known or revered as his cool and methodical friend Scharnhorst, Gneisenau forced the Prussian army to change intellectually just as Scharnhorst had caused it to change structurally. Together the two men broke with the past and institutionalized a new leadership philosophy. Scharnhorst created the structure of the General Staff. But Gneisenau, the charismatic leader and battlefield hero, instituted the fundamental changes in thinking that would change the Prussian way of war. Thus, the philosophy of *Führen durch Auftrag* became the foundation of the new infantry, cavalry, and artillery manuals written after Waterloo.

From the end of the Napoleonic Wars to the appearance of Moltke as the Chief of General Staff in 1857, the newly developed system was expanded and consolidated. Schools sought and enrolled a higher quality of officer candidate. Better-trained officers meant better leadership. Each year, the General Staff recruited only a handful of the best candidates from the new schools. The establishment was small, and with so few General Staff officers in the army, the organization could afford to be highly selective – and it was. The *Allgemeine Kriegsschule* continued to be the breeding ground for aspiring General Staff officers. The three-year course in Berlin, for specially selected officers, was unique. Initially at least, there were no special instructors. The General Staff officers in Berlin would do double duty and instruct the officers for part of the year. Since, by definition, all the officers on the General Staff understood all the staff functions, it was relatively simple to call upon any officer serving on the staff to go over to the school and give instruction. During the campaigning season, the students were sent to the army corps to serve as apprentice staff officers and thereby gain practical experience under the watchful eyes of the various Chiefs of Staff. In this way, the ideas and ethos introduced by Scharnhorst and Gneisenau were inculcated into the General Staff and then, through them, into the whole army. General Staff officers continued to be sprinkled throughout the army in key positions. These officers had all received the same training and, regardless of who their nominal immediate superior was, the actual superior of all General Staff officers was the Chief of the General Staff in Berlin. This built a highly trained and distinctive group, a 'band of brothers' to use Horatio Nelson's term, while at the same time, spreading expertise, and a new leadership philosophy, throughout the army. In 1821, in recognition of their growing *Korpsgeist*, these officers received their own distinctive uniform insignia, which are worn to this day.

The years immediately after the Congress of Vienna were difficult both for Prussia and its army. After the defeat of Napoleon, there was a predictable reactionary period during which most of the reforms were either quashed or reduced in their effectiveness. "The national and progressive ideas of the wars of liberation were crushed by the particularist and retrogressive forces of the age of Metternich."[15] In 1819, Boyen, who had been minister of war since 1813 and who had appointed Grolman as Chief of the General Staff in 1816, resigned over the issue of incorporating the *Landwehr* into the regular army. Grolman soon followed suit. Scharnhorst was dead. Gneisenau had resigned in 1816. Stein had been forced out earlier. With Grolman's resignation, General Rühle von Lilienstern had been made Chief of Staff. Lilienstern was the son of an ennobled officer from Frankfort and had been a pupil of Scharnhorst. In 1821, *Freiherr* von Müffling, a staunch conservative, replaced him. Müffling, although now branded as a reactionary, had been Gneisenau's Senior Staff Officer when they had worked with Blücher, so he was not totally against the new ideas. Clausewitz was the director of the *Allgemeine Kriegsschule*, having been appointed in 1818. Although some of the driving force had been lost, the interplay among these men would keep the doctrine and the ideas alive during the difficult years and national crises that lay ahead. Upon von Müffling's retirement in 1829, General Wilhelm von Krauseneck, who had begun his service in the ranks, was appointed to the post. General Karl von Rheyer replaced him in 1848. Despite the relative rapid succession of Chiefs of the General Staff, and the constraints sometimes put upon them, the officers within the organization continued in the tradition of their founders – at least in terms of military professionalism. There was an unbroken intellectual chain from Scharnhorst to Moltke. All the early Chiefs of Staff were either associates or protégés of their predecessors.

In this way, the Staff had maintained a continuous chain of ideology. The General Staff being small, this continuity was relatively easy to accomplish. In 1822, the Chief of the General Staff, von Müffling, established wargames for all General Staff students. Soon thereafter, regular staff rides (exercises conducted in the field where officers were given tactical problems with only limited information, after which they were required to create plans and orders as they would do in battle), and wargames became the norm for all Prussian officers as part of their pursuit of military excellence. Although all of the Chiefs of General Staff had been given patents of nobility, Scharnhorst's dream of an officer corps based upon an 'aristocracy of merit' had nearly come to pass.

Perhaps no other officer is so closely associated with the concept of *Auftragstaktik* as is Helmuth von Moltke. Although commonly credited with its invention, as we have seen, that is not true. This officer, who never commanded troops in the field above company level, demonstrated that his genius was in the advancement of the concepts that he had been given. He had been a student at the *Allgemeine Kriegsschule* from 1823 to 1826 while Clausewitz was the director. Although it is unlikely that they ever met, the latter's influence upon Moltke was indisputable. Moltke cited *On War* as one of the five most influential books of his life–even if he misinterpreted parts of it.[16] To many, Moltke is most famous for the stunning Prussian victories in the three short and dramatically successful wars during his tenure as Chief of the General Staff. More importantly, "the overwhelming success of his victories against Denmark [1864], Austria [1866], and France [1870-71] encouraged the development of a self-stylized, uniquely German approach to war in the last third of the 19th century."[17] However, Moltke's legacy was far more important than simple military victories. He gave the General Staff a new intellectual impetus. As a disciple of Clausewitz, he saw the need to train officers in an open, and less prescriptive, style of fighting.[18]

Moltke is credited with coining the phrase that is heard in every Western staff college: no plan survives initial contact with the enemy (*Kein Plan überlebt die erste Feindberührung*). He strongly supported the Clausewitzian view that the moral plane was more important than the physical and that uncertainty, friction, and chance all played key roles in achieving victory. As a result of his studies of Napoleon III's 1859 Italian campaign against the Austrians, he became convinced of the need to decentralize control to those levels where commanders could accurately read the battle. "He reasoned that war, a product of opposing wills subject to a host of frictions, gives rise to rapidly changing situations that quickly render a commander's decisions obsolete. Hence, subordinates had to think and act according to the situation, even without or in defiance of orders."[19]

This was not to say that Moltke condoned disobedience. He did not. Moltke monitored subordinate formations closely, and he would issue new directives or dispatch new troops if subordinates strayed from their original purpose. What he espoused was the understanding by all officers that an order given by a superior might easily be rendered irrelevant by circumstance. The enemy, after all, was not privy to the plan. In such cases, the officer responsible to carry out the order had a moral responsibility to alter the plan in such a way as to best achieve the intent of his superior (*Absicht des obergeordneten Führers*). This was not the same as subordinates being allowed to ignore orders – Prussian discipline remained famously strict. This seeming contradiction was the continuing evolution of Gneisenau's *Führen durch Auftrag*, which eventually came to be known as *Auftragstaktik*. To be sure, Moltke's influence was enormous, going far beyond the legitimization of *Auftragstaktik*. His military thinking dominated the Prusso-German school, not only during the latter half of the 19th century, but also well into this century.[20] He made many technical as well as tactical improvements to both the General Staff and to the army as a whole. From the aspect of intellectual revitalization, however, his interpretation and espousal of centralized control through decentralized execution, as well as a more flexible style of warfare, coupled with the control of how this was taught and practised throughout the army, was arguably his greatest achievement.

✠ ✠ ✠

This has been a fleeting chronological view of the intellectual development of *Auftragstaktik*. For reasons of space, large gaps in the history of the Prussian and the German armies have had to be left open. Just the same, the major milestones were covered. Beginning with the revolution in military affairs wrought by the revolutionary wars of the last third of the 18th century, the evolution of Prussian military art was traced in broad terms. The devastating effect of the Prussian defeat at the twin battles of Jena and Auerstädt and the subsequent reform of the army was investigated. Along with the many fundamental structural changes brought about by men like Scharnhorst, Gneisenau, Clausewitz, *et al*, came the more important philosophical changes in how war was to be viewed and battles fought.

Beginning with Scharnhorst, a small group of highly trained and technically proficient officers were given increased responsibility to improve the war fighting capability of the Prussian army. With the rise of Gneisenau came the uniquely Prussian concept of *Führen durch Auftrag* and *Absicht des obergeordneten Führers*. Likewise, Gneisenau introduced the idea of shared responsibility between Commander and Chief of Staff. Clausewitz, although only spoken of in the margins, carried the influence of his original mentor, and institutionalized this influence in his seminal work *On War*. This, in turn, went on to influence men like Moltke, who over a brilliant military career spanning an incredible seven decades, was able to develop and legitimize the original concepts of *Führen durch Auftrag* and *Absicht des obergeordneten Führers*, into the modern concept of *Auftragstaktik*.

NOTES

[1] Hajo Holborn, "The Prusso-German School: Moltke and the Rise of the General Staff" in *Makers of Modern Strategy: from Machiavelli to The Nuclear Age*, Peter Paret, ed., (Princeton NJ, 1986), p.281.

[2] Howard, *European History*, pp.86-87.

[3] Matthew Cooper, *The German Army 1933-1945*, (New York, 1984), p.6, citing Berghan, The Approach of the First World War, (London, 1973), p. 10.

[4] Herbert Pollman, ed. *Lesebuch zur Deutschen Geschichte Band II*, (Berlin,1984), p.184. Translation mine. Emphasis added.

[5] Gordon, A. Craig, *The Politics of the Prussian Army 1640-1945*, (Oxford, 1955), p.44.

[6] Oscar von Lettow-Vorbeck, *Der Krieg*, (Berlin 1893), p.51 as cited in Dirk W. Oetting *Auftragstaktik: Geschichte und Gegenwart einer Führungskonzeption*, (Frankfurt am Main, 1993), p. 49.

[7] Dupuy, pp. 35-36.

[8] Hans von Seeckt, *Thoughts of a Soldier*, Translated by Gilbert Waterhouse, (London, 1930), p.110.

[9] Combined Arms Theory was and remains the central pillar of modern German doctrine, as it is for all of the world's armies. This theory maintains that it is practically impossible to build combat power unless the various arms (infantry, artillery, and cavalry, etc.) are combined in a single formation, i.e. a division.

[10] Craig, *The Prussian Army*, p. 45.

[11] Walter Görlitz, *History of the German General Staff 1657-1945*. Translated by Brian Battershaw, (New York, 1961), p.27.

[12] Millotat, *Understanding the General System*, (Carlisle Barracks, PA, 1992), p. 27. A Führergehilfe is a unique mix of advisor, co-commander, and personal assistant. I experienced this relationship firsthand while serving as the *Führergehilfe* to the Commander of Panzerbrigade 12 for a large field training exercise in the fall of 1987. At one point, even though I was a Canadian major, I had operational command of the brigade for the better part of a full day in the commander's absence.

[13] *Ibid*, The idea of shared responsibility, a uniquely German relationship between

Commander and Chief of Staff. This relationship is little understood outside of Germany and lies at the core of *Auftragstaktik*.

[14] Hans Delbrück, *Das Leben des Feldmarschalls Grafen von Gneisenau*, (Berlin, 1920), and Görlitz, *General Staff*, pp.40-49, as quoted in Millotat, p.31.

[15] Martin Kitchen, *A Military History of Germany, A Military History of Germany from the eighteenth century to the present day*, (London, 1975), p.62.

[16] Eberhard Kessel, *Moltke*, (Stuttgart, 1957), p.108 as cited by Antulio J. Echevarria II in "Moltke and the German Military Tradition: His Theories and Legacies," *Parameters*, Spring 1996, p.92.

[17] Echevarria. "Military Tradition", p.96.

[18] Moltke himself referred to himself in this way. See also Jehuda Wallach, *Das Dogma der Vernichtungsschlacht*, (Frankfurt, 1967) and Roland Foerster, "Operational Thinking of the Elder Moltke and its Consequences", in *Operational Thinking in Clausewitz, Moltke, Schlieffen and Manstein*, (Bonn, 1988).

[19] Echevarria, "Military Tradition," p.97.

[20] Gunther Rothenberg, "Moltke, Schlieffen, and the Doctrine of Strategic Envelopment" in *Makers of Modern Strategy: from Machiavelli to the Nuclear Age*. Peter Paret, ed., (Princeton, 1986), p. 296.

Feldmarshal Helmuth Graf von Moltke
Photo by F. Brandt

AUFTRAGSTAKTIK

It is best to only give those orders which are absolutely necessary.
                                        - **Graf Helmuth von Moltke**

he interaction of ideas and organizations is a field of study all its own. How any large organization like the Great General Staff, is structured plays an important role in how it conducts its business. Likewise, ideas are either both accepted and fostered or rejected and belittled because of how the organization is put together. Professor Showalter offers an apt description of what occurred in the Prussian army after the French Revolution: "Scholars and soldiers alike tend to denigrate the role of organizations in fostering change ... But internal structures, human dynamics, and a sense of purpose all influence the uses made of new and old tools of war."[1] New ideas were introduced into a structure, the Prussian army, which placed little value on these ideas. Despite this dislike of new ideas, the structure of the army was forced to change. In turn, this change allowed some of these new ideas to take hold, grow, and to be fostered. The result was a re-evaluation by the Prussians of the nature of war and warfare; what these concepts meant to Prussia and to the army, and in what manner they should best be translated into action.

The entire history of the development of *Auftragstaktik* revolves around one simple question: How did the Prussian army view war? All other issues, however interesting or important, are secondary to this pivotal philosophical question. From an intellectual perspective, the simple answer was what Dupuy called the institutionalization of chaos in battle.[2] This concept encapsulated all aspects of *Kriegskunst*: From Gneisenau's *Auftragstaktik* to Scharnhorst's *Generalstab* to Moltke's minimalist approach to orders, commanders would be well served "only to give those orders which are absolutely necessary."[3] The conviction that war was a violent, chaotic, irrational, and uncontrollable human activity was, and remains to this day, the most identifiable embodiment of the Prusso-German school of war.[4] While other armies strove to bring parade-square order to the battlefield, the Prussian army ensconced the Clausewitzian concepts of chaos and friction into its tactical doctrine.

By no means is this to say that Prussian tactics were chaotic. On the contrary, the use of rigid discipline and effective battle drills gave Prussian commanders at all levels the potential to exploit the ever-changing face of battle. The great paradox of Prussian discipline was that precision drill and unquestioning obedience could instil initiative and independence at all levels, from infantry section to army group. Before Prussian soldiers could be expected to exercise their initiative, they had to be psychologically prepared to act independently and to accept the utter confusion, which Clausewitz had taught was the normal situation in combat. This was *fundamentally* different from what all other armies were training their soldiers and leaders to do. The idea of military drill, whether it was the Macedonian *phalanx* or the British thin red line, was that a commander needed to impose order upon disorder. The key to Prussian victory was not to attempt to impose order on chaos but, rather, to take maximum advantage of this chaos and to manipulate it for tactical advantage. The concept was both elementary and ancient. Although the Prussian army did not give up battle drills, officers and soldiers were allowed the freedom to act as they needed in accordance with their local situations.

The Prussian army had not always perceived battle in this way; it had not always embraced chaos. Its acceptance of the concept can be traced to the French Revolution. The military societies of this era were openly discussing new tactics, new leadership, and the idea of giving individual soldiers more freedom to act. Pre-Revolutionary armies, as epitomized by the Prussians under Frederick the Great, had worked diligently at perfecting battlefield drill movements. Under Frederick the Great, the Prussian army had been a formidable force precisely because of Frederick's genius in the application of this battlefield drill. When Napoleon changed warfare by demonstrating his mastery of 'battlespace dominance' what he was doing was applying, in his own unique manner, his new interpretation of battlefield drills. When Napoleon's intent was understood and applied, as with the ruthless pursuit of the Prussian army to the Baltic after the Battle of Jena, crushing victories ensued.[5] It was this unique, and pivotal, interpretation that Scharnhorst, Gneisenau, Clausewitz and Moltke had grasped and then, using the General Staff as the medium, institutionalized it in the Prussian army.

☩ ☩ ☩

Consider organizational structures. Armies, like all corporate bodies, can be considered to have a tripartite structure comprising mind, body, and soul. The mind of an army concerns doctrine, strategy, and tactics. The body comprises its structures, organizations, and chains of command. The soul encompasses its élan, *esprit de corps,* or, in the case of the German Army, *Korpsgeist*, as represented by its people. In Prussia's case, Frederick the Great had been the mind of his army. His tactical brilliance and the strategic use of his troops had made his country a military power out of all proportion to its size and national wealth. In his case, there was little question of an army doctrine or strategy. Although Frederick did write a book describing his views on how to fight, the Prussian army and its regiments were very much his personal possessions. Further, the relationship between the army and the king was more than personal; it was deeply feudal, and Frederick's view of warfare did not include giving subordinates freedom of action.

After Frederick's death, for Prussian soldiers to translate the Clausewitzian understanding of the nature of war into action and to exploit chaos, a critical new precondition was needed. Exploiting chaos through *Auftragstaktik* required the leadership philosophy, or 'command climate' in the Prussian army to change such that soldiers at all levels felt they had the freedom to act as the situation dictated. Independence had to be balanced against the need to obey orders and maintain discipline. This was no simple task and, of course, was inextricably linked to the non-military complexities of self-image, socio-economic, and civil-military relationships, among manifold other factors. Certainly, such change would take time. Any army, which had been based on iron discipline and the lash, was not about to embrace independent action overnight.

Immediately after the humiliation at Jena, Scharnhorst and Gneisenau had insisted on the teaching of Napoleon's successful pursuit in the *Allgemeine Kriegsschule*. Later, in the aftermath of Waterloo, Blücher and Gneisenau pushed hard to pursue the retreating French into Paris. But *wünschen heißt nicht können* – wishing does not make it so. Although the Prussians had been taught the importance of independent action, they only pursued the retreating French aggressively when pushed by Blücher or his Chief of Staff. Senior Prussian commanders demonstrated very little initiative. None the less, Blücher and Gneisenau were relentless, and the French were denied the ability to take up defensive positions in front of Paris. Success in instilling initiative was limited; but, compared with what the army had looked like in 1806, less than a decade before, there was the promise of better performance to come.

The intellectual changes and the introduction of new ideas ushered in by the French Revolution into the 19th century Prussian army had created new tools of warfare. Among them was a particularly intellectual tool, one that had the innate power to allow the Prussian army to harness and exploit the very nature of war. Gneisenau embraced this intellectual change. He was a much more charismatic and impetuous personality than was his predecessor. Having had experience in America as a mercenary under the British, he understood the impact that the new skirmishing tactics could have upon low-level tactics. "It was in America that he learnt at first hand the lessons of the importance of sharpshooting and of high morale, and he was determined to instil some of the same enthusiasm and fervour into the Prussians."[6] The intellectual parent of *Auftragstaktik*, therefore, was Gneisenau.

He was the first to develop command and control by directives, thus giving latitude to the subordinate commanders for the execution of operations. Subordinate commanders were for the first time issued directives expressing the intent of the royal headquarters in terms of clear objectives but with only general indications of the methods of their achievement. This enabled commanders and their General Staff officers to use initiative in taking advantage of unforeseen opportunities, provided that their actions were consistent with the main objective. Thus, Gneisenau laid the cornerstone of the German leadership philosophy: mission-oriented command and control.

Gneisenau's new philosophy had been an outgrowth of many factors. Further, not all the senior Prussian commanders were enamoured of this philosophy. Gneisenau, like his comrades Scharnhorst and Clausewitz, had been observing and discussing French tactics for years. It would be fair, therefore, to classify his philosophy as a synthesis of the Napoleonic ideals of *l'intention du Commandant* and *liberté d'action* with his own personal combat experience. In the end, Gneisenau was able to institute his ideas and even enshrine them into tactical doctrine to the extent that many of his views on war and its conduct, just like those of his friend Clausewitz, are still to be found in today's *Bundeswehr* regulations and tactical manuals.

These philosophic, or attitudinal, changes could not have survived without the necessary structures to support them. Despite initial difficulties, the introduction of French formations such as the army division, in 1806, had been of enormous benefit.[7] More useful, though, were the manifold changes made by Scharnhorst's restructuring of the Staff and the army. Wrought in conjunction with Gneisenau's intellectual changes, these structural changes likewise had enormous potential to alter Prussia's warfighting style. Scharnhorst, in great measure, built the mechanisms whereby the conceptual tools could be used to maximum effect. For instance, he restructured the army's educational system, he posted selected General Staff officers to all field formations, and he subordinated all General Staff officers to the Chief of the General Staff. All of these changes, combined with the new thinking, created the idea that eventually grew to become the very heart of German *Kriegskunst*: the idea of *Auftragstaktik*.

As already noted, after the peace in 1815, there was reluctance in Prussia to institute the lessons that the preceding decade had taught. The officer corps demonstrated a desire to return to the halcyon days before Napoleon and before the Reform Commission had begun its work. The longing to return to the *status quo ante* was fought by the surviving reformers. Scharnhorst's General Staff, with Gneisenau as its Chief, put up the greatest defence of the reforms. After Gneisenau's departure, the operating principles of the Staff, as well as the wargames and procedures introduced by von Müffling and his replacement, General von Krauseneck, finally established the General Staff as the guiding organ of the Prussian army. The extent to which the officer corps had stagnated after the initial reforms remains moot.[8]

Certainly, there was some retrenching by the conservative elements, but the entry of non-aristocratic candidates into the officers' ranks continued, and with them came liberal ideas and attitudes. However, despite a growing acceptance of these liberal ideas, the officer corps continued to bind itself ever more closely with the person of the king.[9] It is this period in which we see the origins of the uniquely Prussian dichotomy of strict obedience combined with independent thought.

The growth of the army's acceptance of initiative and independent thought is not unusual when seen within the broader background of German culture. Germany was undergoing a cultural expansion in terms of art, philosophy, and the understanding of the individual in society. Across Europe the 1848 social agitations pushed governments for reform. Although a time of political stagnation in the German states, it was nonetheless the golden "age of German literature and philosophy, the age of Goethe and Schiller, of Kant, Fichte, and Hegel, of Herder and Schleiermacher, Tieck and Novalis, the Schlegels, and the Humboldts."[10] In the army, by the 1840s, serious concern was finally being given to the rewriting and updating of the field tactical manuals and regulations – many of which had not been revised since 1788. This review was spurred by a quiet but growing debate on the question of obedience versus individual initiative. A new regulation written in 1837, Regulation Number 7, stated in Paragraph 40 that any soldier receiving an order, which was either impossible to execute, unjust, or which had no hope of achieving the commander's intent, was immediately to report to his superior that he could not accept the order.[11] This new paragraph acted as a brake on illegal action and became the basis for subsequent inquiries. How did the army deal with this seeming contradiction between loyalty and initiative? It further developed the army's understanding of the basis for *Auftragstaktik*.

In simple terms, subordinates were being trained to act independently. They were being empowered to make decisions at their own levels of influence. This empowerment created a *chain of initiative*. The nature of battle being chaotic, subordinate leaders down to the youngest squad leader were empowered to make independent decisions and to take action that would contribute to tactical success. The effect of this chain of initiative was that commanders in the field gained enormous *Freiheit des Handelns* – freedom of action. At all levels, leaders were to be imbued with the will of the commander – even if it meant acting in a manner that ostensibly seemed to run counter to orders.

By mid-century, Gneisenau's ideas had taken a firm hold. Prince Frederick Charles, nephew of Frederick Wilhelm IV, a life-long soldier and General Staff officer, wrote extensively on the issue of independent thought and action in the army. Born in 1828, he has been credited with being a significant influence on Prussian tactical doctrine; he was active in the army and commanded the Prussian forces in the 1864 war with Denmark. In an 1851 essay, he reminded all soldiers that "Independence is a virtue, without which one cannot become a good field soldier."[12] In other words, not only did Prussian soldiers have a *right* to be independent thinkers, but they also had an *obligation* to be so. In 1860, in another essay, he expressed his convictions again. Without using the word, the prince's philosophy lays the foundation of *Auftragstaktik*:

> Prussian officers object to being hemmed in by rules and regulations, like officers in Russia, Austria, and England. With officers like ours you cannot fight a formal defensive action of the kind that Wellington introduced, whereby every individual is bound by rules and procedures. We look at the way things tend to go and leave the individual more freedom to use initiative; we ride him on a looser rein, back up each separate success even if it had run counter to the intentions of a commander-in-chief such as Wellington, who used to insist on having full control over every unit at all times. But that you cannot have if subordinate commanders, without the knowledge or instructions of their seniors, go off into action on their own, exploiting each and every advantage, as they do with us.[13]

It is not possible to discuss the Prussian army in the latter half of the 19th century without mentioning the great influence of technology upon the army and its way of war. The question of the relationship between technology and warfare is as old as war itself, and it continues to be discussed in every staff college in the world. That technology has had a great influence upon warfare, particularly in the 19th century, is unquestioned; but technological development must be seen more as a facilitating factor than as a decisive one. Since *Auftragstaktik* had arisen in an earlier age, it is highly likely that, with or without the advent of telegraphs, railroads, or needle guns, the Prussian leadership philosophy would have continued to develop in the direction of *Auftragstaktik*. This is not to say that technology was not critically important to the Prussian way of war, for obviously it was. However, by the latter half of the century, the ideas of independent action, commander's intent, and *Führen durch Auftrag*, were well established and their influence felt for some time.

In the same way that the General Staff had found its greatest leader in the person of Moltke, so too was this extraordinary individual perhaps the greatest practitioner of *Auftragstaktik*. Moltke's genius was not founded on his combat experience as a senior commander. This seemingly crippling disadvantage was turned to advantage by his understanding that the critical function of senior commanders was the formulation of a campaign-winning plan. In his case, he would translate the plan into directives (*Weisungen*) and then give these directives to the army's corps commanders. The field commanders would then, on their own, translate the directives into missions within the context of the superior commanders' intent (*Absicht des obergeordneten Führers*), using one of the techniques that Moltke introduced: keeping orders as short as possible with nothing in the order except that which was fully necessary. (*Nicht mehr befehlen als durchaus nötig*). He standardized orders for field operations and strove to keep them as short and simple as he could. This allowed subordinates to analyse their orders (*Auswertung*) and, hence, gave them the freedom to decide how best to achieve the superior commander's intent.[14]

In this case, the superior commander was Moltke, acting on behalf of the king. The Chief of the General Staff had the king's every confidence, to the extent that the monarch issued a brief but momentous edict in 1866 giving his Chief of General Staff *carte blanche* to send directives, on his behalf, directly to the army corps. This action allowed Moltke to issue orders without first getting royal approval. During the Prusso-Danish War in 1864, Moltke had had no direct contact with or authority over the army's field commander. By the time Prussia was preparing to fight its great rival Austria, the situation had changed. On 2 June 1866:

> ...a royal order provided for the communication of commands directly from the general staff to the troops, rather than through the Ministry of War. When peace came, the general staff again became subordinate to the Ministry. Nonetheless, the first step had been taken that would lead one day to its liberation from all ministerial authority.[15]

This simple change brought enormous benefits. Not only did it allow Moltke to monitor and influence the battles, it also gave him the freedom to allow more initiative to commanders in the field with the understanding that these commanders would do likewise with their own subordinates.

Moltke made no attempts to control detailed aspects of any engagement. His strength lay in his ability to bring his commanders together at the right time and place, arm them with the necessary tools and concepts, and then give them the freedom of action to accomplish their missions:

> Moltke probably did not think that Prussian commanders, all indoctrinated with a common adherence to the concept of offensive warfare, would have been as indecisive as their French and Austrian counterparts, but he was determined to do what he could to avoid any such possibility. The examples of the Italian Campaign reaffirmed his view that commanders should be assigned general missions, related to fundamental, clearly understood objectives, and then instructed to accomplish those missions by carrying the fight aggressively to the enemy. It was also evident to him that the old Napoleonic precept, 'Separate to live, unite to fight' needed to be slightly updated for the larger armies of the mid-19th century: 'Separate to *live and to move*; unite *only* to fight'. [16]

This paradoxical notion was not easy for all to grasp, and there were instances where subordinate commanders did not fully understand. To reinforce this seeming contradiction of acting in accordance with commander's intent – even to the extent of disobedience – a story, perhaps apocryphal, made the rounds in the army at the time of the Austro-Prussian War. *Prinz* Frederick Charles, an innovative and educated career officer who commanded the First Army against the Austrians, was chastising a battalion commander for a tactical blunder. In his own defence, the officer stated that he was merely following orders. The prince reputedly retorted that 'His Majesty made you a major because he believed you would know when *not* to obey his orders.' Whether true or not, the essence of the dilemma highlighted the apparent dichotomy of Prussian leadership. This dichotomy went on to become a guiding principle for generations of Prussian, and thereafter, all German officers.

Moltke considered the matter of officers being decisive as critical. Since the reforms and revitalized teachings of Scharnhorst and Gneisenau, the necessity of not waiting for orders had been continually emphasized and Moltke reinforced the Clausewitzian attitude of the necessity for moral fortitude in the confusion of battle. The need to be decisive was paramount and could not be hampered by waiting for orders from superiors. He stressed the need for all commanders to carry out the will of their superiors (*der Willen seines Vorgesetzten*); and he personally inserted the following paragraph into the Prussian doctrinal manuals (and it was still in the tactical manuals when I attended the *FüAk*): 'A favourable situation will never be exploited if commanders wait for orders. The highest commander and the youngest soldier must always be conscious of the fact that omission and inactivity are worse than resorting to the wrong expedient.' During his extraordinary tenure as Chief of Staff, Moltke brought together the drive for independent action, which was being called for by Prince Frederick Charles, and the need for strong discipline within the chain of command, which had been the Prussian tradition since before Frederick the Great.

Thus, the early work of Scharnhorst and his reformers had come to fruition under the tutelage of Moltke during his long term as Chief of the Great General Staff. When Scharnhorst had written that "the physical agility and high intelligence of the common man enables the French *tirailleurs* to profit from all advantages offered by the terrain and the general situation, while the phlegmatic Germans, Bohemians, and Dutch form on open ground and do nothing but what their officer orders them to do,"[17] one might imagine that he hoped for a time when the situation would be better. The Prussian General Staff that Scharnhorst created became the vehicle for that betterment. Initially, under the influence of Gneisenau's new tactical philosophy, the Staff began to realize Scharnhorst's vision. Later, the Staff would further develop the ideas of these two men and would be additionally molded by Clausewitz's teachings and his doctrine of "the bloody vigor of war."[18]

⊞ ⊞ ⊞

With no small irony, the deeply Clausewitzian Prussian army achieved its Clausewitzian "culminating point"[19] under the skillful tutelage of Helmuth von Moltke. The ideas of Scharnhorst, but especially those of Gneisenau, firmly established the Prusso-German school of war. But it was under Moltke, who appreciated the delicate balance that needed to be struck among independent thought and action, the commander's intent, and the immediate military situation facing every soldier on the battlefield, that the hoped-for apogee was achieved. Writing a decade before the First World War, R. Friedrich in his official history of Moltke's tenure as Chief of Staff, made it clear:

> The Gneisenaun understanding of the duties and responsibilities of the General Staff, of its means and method of performing these duties, have remained in effect, practically unchanged, to this day. They have led to the great victories of 1866 and 1870 and have given the Prussian General Staff the great reputation, which it everywhere today enjoys.[20]

The early work of the reformers had come to full fruit. The structures created to save a once proud army after a humiliating defeat had become well established. Scharnhorst had wrenched the Prussian army from its outdated paradigm and laid the foundations for future excellence.

Those who followed him built upon his foundations. Gneisenau gave the army the French concept of commander's intent and adapted it to fit the Prussian philosophy. The General Staff perpetuated itself until Moltke could take the helm and further refine the ideas of Scharnhorst and Gneisenau. By the time Prussia and its army helped to create the German *Reich*, the idea of independent action and working within the analysis of a directive given to an officer by his superior was firmly embedded in the Prussian military psyche. Although by this stage it had not yet received its modern name, there could be little doubt that the Prussian way of war had been entrenched as what is today called *Auftragstaktik*.

NOTES

[1] Dennis E. Showalter, "Prussia, Technology and War: Artillery From 1815-1914", in *Men Machines and War*, R. Haycock and K. Neilson eds., (Waterloo, ON, 1988), p.117.

[2] T. N. Dupuy, *A Genius for War: The German Army and General Staff, 1807-1945*, (Englewood Cliffs NJ, 1977), p. 103.

[3] From Moltke's *Verordnung für die höheren Truppenführer*, which the Chief of Staff issued 24 June 1869, as found in Dirk W. Oetting *Auftragstaktik: Geschichte und Gegenwart einer Führungskonzeption*, (Frankfurt am Main, 1993), p.104. Translated by me.

[4] My personal experience, during the two-year General Staff course in the *Führungsakademie*, was that this aspect of German warfare was the most elusive for most foreign officers to grasp. Foreign officers, and particularly those from Anglo-Saxon backgrounds, had difficulty in appreciating the depth of conviction that *Bundeswehr* officers have that this Clausewitzian view of war is correct.

[5] Dupuy, pp. 35-36.

[6] Martin Kitchen, *A Military History of Germany, A Military History of Germany from the eighteenth century to the present day*, (London, 1975), p.57.

[7] Walter O. Shanahan, *Prussian Military Reforms 1786 –1813*, (New York, 1945), pp.85-86.

[8] Karl Demeter, *The German Officer-Corps in Society and State 1650 -1945*, translated by Angus Malcolm, (London, 1965), p.251.

[9] Oetting, p.85.

[10] R.R. Palmer, *The World of the French Revolution*, (New York, 1971), p.234.

[11] Oetting, p.88. Oetting goes on to state that this order has remained in effect in the *Bundeswehr* up to the present day. For example, in May 1944, as the Canadian army broke through the German defence on the Melfa River, General Feurstein reported to his superior Gen von Vietinghoff that his order to defend was untenable. The Corps Operations Officer recorded the conversation as an "Official Note Fact" for use in any subsequent official inquiries. See Michael P. Cessford "Warriors for the Working Day", Unpublished PhD dissertation, (Carleton University, 1996) , pp.73-74. This idea serves as the basis of what is now called *Innere Führung*, a post-1945 concept that is one of the new foundations of the *Bundeswehr*. Although complex, the idea is simple in principle and is designed to avoid the atrocities visited upon the army by the Nazis.

[12] Essay entitled "Selbständiges Denken und Handeln", as quoted in Oetting, p.98. "Selbständigkeit ist eine Tugend, ohne die kein guten Feldsoldat gedacht werden kann." Translated by me.

[13] Essay by Prince Frederick Charles of Prussia on "the origins and Development of the Spirit of the Prussian Officer, its Manifestations and its Effect", 3 January 1860, as quoted in Demeter, pp. 260-261.

[14] Moltke's influence is felt to this day. At the *FüAk*, how well a commander's intent could be analyzed and translated into a concise and standard order was, and continues to be, the hallmark of truly professional staff work.

[15] Otto Planze, *Bismarck and the Development of Germany, Volume I, 1815-1879*, (Princeton, 1990), p. 363.

[16] Dupuy, p. 67.

[17] Palmer, *French Revolution*, p. 119.

[18] Gerhard Ritter, *The Sword and the Scepter, The Problem of Militarism in Germany, Vol I 1740 –1890*, (Coral Gables FL, 1969), p.60.

[19] The concept of a culminating point (*Kulminationspunkt*) was first conceived of by Clausewitz (Book VII, Chapter 5). It is the point at which an attacking force can no longer proceed, a high-water mark.

[20] R. Friederich, *Erzieher des Preußischen Heeres Band 6 – Gneisenau*, (Berlin, 1906), p. 118. Translated by me.

Generaloberst Johannes "Hans" Friedrich Leopold von Seeckt
Photographer unknown

INTERREGNUM, BLITZKRIEG UND HUBRIS

We are still too near the events to be able to judge them without passion. But one must take into account the extremely difficult position of the chief soldiers of the 'Third Reich'. They had to carry through their struggles of conscience quite alone, without being able to seek advice from members of parliament, from a free Press, or from any other responsible and independent men.

- General Siegfried Westphal

he study of the creation of German leadership's most effective tool formally stopped before the dawning of the First World War. The reasons for this halt were several. Foremost among them were that the concept was by then fully formed and the war was the antithesis of the German military concept of *Bewegungskrieg* or war of movement, which was so connected to the concept of *Auftragstaktik*, leaving sharply limited opportunity for independent thought or freedom of action. Nonetheless, the deeply ingrained leadership philosophy remained and continued to function as part of the warp and weft of the fabric of German military thought and practice. Proof of this claim was the army's institutional conduct after the war was lost, the professionalism that drove the investigation of its defeat, and the subsequent preparation for any potential renewal of hostilities. It is to this conduct that we now briefly turn.

The concept of *hubris* has been passed on to us by the ancient Greeks and classical literature from the *Iliad* to *Beowulf* to Mary Shelly's *Frankenstein*. These tales are replete with stories of overweening men who believed that they could not fail. These stories are of individuals, products of their cultures, who went astray and, in classical Greek lore, tempted the gods and destroyed themselves. What more fitting analogy could there be to describe what befell Germany when it was held in thrall by Adolf Hitler and his fellow Nazi madmen as he marched the nation towards its Wagnerian *Götterdämmerung*, its Twilight of the Gods?

The two decades separating the Armistice in November of 1918 and the German occupation of the Czech Sudetenland in September of 1938 is one of those extraordinary periods in history that are difficult to define. For many, the two world wars of the 20th century can easily be seen as a single conflict since the first war was in many ways a precondition for the second. To some, 1914 to 1945 delineates a Second Thirty Years' War. Viewed in this light, the twenty years in question were an interregnum or hiatus. The two-decade pause brought upheaval and renewal from the Atlantic Ocean to the Russian Steppes. While Europe struggled to recover from the loss of an entire generation of young men and economies pivoted away from war production to the creation of wealth and consumer goods, the ex-belligerents' militaries studied the four years of war to attempt to tease out valuable lessons. Several schools of thought emerged from this study, but none were as analytical or as well-considered as was conducted in Germany.

In Britain, France, Germany, Italy, and the newly established Soviet Union, men like Basil Liddell Hart, JFC Fuller, Heinz Guderian, Charles de Gaulle, and Mikhail Tukhachevsky embraced machine warfare and the vision of returning mobility to the battlefield. Others like Billy Mitchell and Hugh Trenchard became convinced that Giulio Douhet, Italy's father of aerial warfare, had found the answer to obviating the insanity of trench warfare. Regardless of their country, their arm of service or their rank, all were roundly criticized as being fabulists. Some of their claims were prophetic; many were absurd.

For Germany, the punitive Treaty of Versailles dismembered the defeated *Reichswehr*. More than just demobilizing the German military, it placed severe constraints upon its existence and sought to severely constrain its development or modernization. The Great General Staff was disbanded and outlawed. The *Reichsheer* was limited to 100,000 all ranks of which no more than 4,000 were to be commissioned officers. This was an army smaller than Denmark's, Belgium's, or Poland's and it was an army forbidden to have tanks of any kind. The *Luftwaffe* was outlawed. The *Kaiserliche Marine* was disbanded, reformed as the *Reichsmarine,* limited to 15,000 all ranks, and to consist of no more than six battleships, six light cruisers, 12 destroyers, and 12 torpedo boats. Submarines, like tanks, were forbidden.

The victors' attempt to stop German military development not only failed; arguably, it was counterproductive. The far-reaching consequences of the changes established in 1821, with the formal creation of the *Generalstab* with *Freiherr* von Müffling at its head now bore fruit in an unanticipated way. As it had done for a century, the General Staff, now reconfigured as the *Heeresamt,* or Army Office, set about systematically revisiting its doctrine, tactics, and training processes under its brilliant chief, General Hans von Seeckt, who had spent most of the war on the more mobile Eastern Front and as chief of staff of the Turkish Army. He returned to Germany in November 1918 to be the last Chief of General Staff before its official disbandment in July of 1919. It was in this last capacity that he had his most lasting influence:

> He completely rewrote the army's manuals and field service regulations; he inaugurated research projects, sometimes in disguised facilities abroad, to keep abreast of new developments in technology; he did everything possible to ensure that his 100,000 men were the best-trained tiny army on the planet. But he also was wise enough not to topple the whole edifice and start over. A veteran of the war's eastern front, he was remarkably immune to the so-called lessons of World War I. To him, they were merely lessons of the aberration that was the western front....[1]

Like so many German General Staff officers before and since, von Seeckt was a disciple of independent thought, freedom of manoeuvre, and of battlefield mobility. He was key in keeping alive a generations-long German concepts of *Auftragstaktik, Bewegungskrieg* and *Freiheit des Handelns.* Moltke the Elder had demonstrated his brilliance using these concepts in his three victories of 1848, 1866, and 1870, and von Seeckt guarded them like sacred flames and, under his leadership and guidance, the *Heeresamt* studied, analyzed, and scrutinized not just the operation and tactics of the war but dissected and refreshed the army's doctrine, training, and processes. Once again, the seeds of a renewed army were planted and awaiting germination.

One of these seeds was the new creation of the armoured division, which saw the concentration of tanks in a single formation supported by an all-arms team that had equivalent mobility. Whether borrowed from the writings of JFC Fuller or the outcome of combining the established concepts of *Auftragstaktik*, *Bewegungskrieg* and *Freiheit des Handelns* is not important here. What is important is what happened when the fruits of von Seeckt's labours were put to the test of battle.

Between 1935 and 1942, Nazi Germany and its military was almost unfailingly successful. Beginning with a unilateral repudiation of the Versailles Treaty and then introducing conscription Hitler, in his maniacal lunge for world domination, made a series of bold and dramatic moves, both political and military. The once utterly prone Germany was once again on the march and invading neighbours and, within two short years, Germany occupied and controlled much of Europe. German military forces met with astonishing success with one swift victory after another. In 1936, Germany occupied and reclaimed the demilitarized Rhineland between France and Germany. In 1937, Germany joined Italy in militarily supporting fascist forces in Spain. In 1938, Germany unilaterally annexed Austria and occupied it. Later that year, Hitler manoeuvred to strip the Sudetenland out of Czechoslovakia and then in 1939 occupied it. Bolstered by the lack of response from England and France, Hitler's successful invasions followed in a rapid and overwhelming succession: Poland in September 1939, Denmark in April 1940, Norway in April 1940, Belgium, the Netherlands, Luxembourg, and France all in May 1940, Yugoslavia, and Greece in April 1941 and finally on 22 June 1941, in an unexpected and apparently unstoppable lunge, invaded his erstwhile ally the Soviet Union. It had been an almost unbelievable succession of victories. It was by no means bloodless, the invasion of Poland, for instance, had cost almost 50,000 soldiers in dead, wounded, and missing. Nonetheless, the string of victories and the territories gained was astounding.

Every winning streak has a turning point and, late in 1941, the tide turned for the *Wehrmacht*. The astounding series of 'lightning' military attacks ground to a halt. The rapid victories ended abruptly. Why? What changed? Why was Germany so successful for so long, but suddenly no longer able to use its *Blitzkrieg* or 'lightning war' tactics? Of course, there is no simple explanation to such a multi-faceted issue. But this question offers an opportunity to demonstrate how the lack of an effective strategy cannot be overcome with even the best of tools and processes.

First, let us consider the reason for German success between 1935 and 1942: Germany, because of Hitler's ability to divide potential opponents, fought a series of short, sharp campaigns rather than a war – campaigns that were isolated from one another by both time and space. These isolated campaigns were directed against individual states – one at a time – and, except for France, these states were greatly inferior to Germany in terms of population, industry, military power, and preparedness. Whereas all the above states, and their armies, had ended the First World War with little or no serious thought for the next war, the German army had spent the interwar years under the tutelage of von Seeckt and his hand-picked cadre of General Staff officers hidden in the *Heeresamt* as they toiled to prepare Germany for the next conflict: a war which would see the tiny *Reichswehr* balloon to become the multi-million-man *Wehrmacht* that would at its height approach 10,000,000 personnel in uniform.

When the Nazis seized power in 1933, the army's leadership was wary of entering another long, drawn-out war. Hitler's political maneuverings reinforced their fears. Von Seeckt, his peers, and those officers trained by them saw that Hitler was creating the national preconditions for a prolonged war – something all the General Staff officers who had fought the last war were eager to avoid. But even as their concerns grew, many allowed themselves to believe that their fabled self-discipline, education, and professionalism would allow them to easily control this erstwhile corporal who had become chancellor.

Germany's tactical and operational successes up to 1942 had taught many false lessons. The short, violent, and rapid campaigns lulled both the military and the political leadership into believing that no country was a match for Germany's might. The difficulty with this strategy was that no operational or strategic concepts underpinned them, a fact that became increasingly obvious on the Eastern Front, in part because the enormous size of the theater demanded an operational level of war, in part because of the fundamental German error of seeking victory in a single decisive battle, and in part because tactical concentration could not produce operational victories. In short, what they were using as a basis for their planning was not a strategy at all.

The hubris that was born of the victories of 1936-42 was ready to blossom once the Japanese attacked Pearl Harbor and the Americans entered the war. General George Catlett Marshall, the American Chief of Staff, correctly foresaw that a long war strategy was the only way that America could hope to win, so he did what every great strategist has done: he forced the enemy to play by his rules. Initially, this long-war strategy did not appear to work. The American military was woefully small and unprepared. As with all long-game strategies, once it took hold, it was a race that only one horse had the legs to win.

It might help to look at this situation not from the strategic or operational or even the tactical perspective. Look at it conceptually. A noted American Clausewitzian scholar, Antulio Echevarria II, put it succinctly when he said that Germany had used *force* instead of *power*. German leadership, both political and military, confused military force with national power (arguably, a mistake that the Americans themselves have made several times in the 20th century). In other words, forgetting that national power has many elements, the Germans confused it with military force, and thereby failed to comprehend the limitations of force within the greater international community. In effect, what the West knew as *Blitzkrieg* was the manifestation of this misunderstanding. Further complicating the misunderstanding was the fact that the German military neither invented nor used this term:

> The German army did not invent it, rarely used it outside of quotation marks, and would never use it to describe either a

general operational doctrine or a specific historical operation. Its origins are obscure, but it apparently first appeared in Western journalistic usage in a 1939 issue of *Time* magazine to describe the lightning-quick German victories of the opening days of World War II.[2]

This form of warfare was a low-level tactical concept, but Hitler, unschooled in military theory, mistook it for a strategy. It might well have been useful as such except that the Nazis did not configure their armed forces to carry out such as strategy. The myth created by *Blitzkrieg* contained the seeds of its own destruction. The more they tried to use it, the worse it became because the short sharp engagements that strove for decisive but elusive ultimate victories used up resources that Germany could ill afford, whereas the Americans and the Soviets could absorb the short-term losses if the long-term strategy made progress. This situation had many parallels with the strategy that Ulysses Grant used to defeat Robert E. Lee, and any serious student of the American Civil War can easily draw the comparisons.

To summarize, the Germans inadvertently got themselves into a long war but only had a playbook that allowed them to fight a succession of short wars, or more correctly, they fought campaigns – most of which they won. The tactical excellence and battle-winning doctrine, even combined with the intellectual horsepower of the General Staff, could not overcome the fact that they lacked an adequate strategy. To paraphrase Vietnamese Colonel Tu when he described why the Americans had lost the Vietnam War, just as the Americans had consistently won their tactical engagements, the fact that the Germans continually outfought the Soviets and the Allies at the tactical level became irrelevant. They had forgotten their Clausewitz.[3]

NOTES

[1] Robert M. Citino, *Quest for Decisive Victory: From Stalemate to Blitzkrieg in Europe, 1899-1940*, (Lawrence, KA: 2002), p. 194.

[2] *Ibid*, p. 181.

[3] Harry G. Summers, Jr., *On Strategy: The Vietnam War in Context*, (Carlisle Barracks, PA, 1983), p. 1.

Feldmarshal Alfred von Schlieffen
Photo Studio E. Bieber 1906

MILITARY DOCTRINE

Nothing so comforts the military mind as the maxim of a great but dead general.

- Barbara W. Tuchman

I f the history of *Auftragstaktik* has taught us anything, it is that this leadership philosophy cannot simply be cut and pasted into our own doctrine. Linked by history and culture to German fighting forces, *Auftragstaktik* does not stand alone as a leadership attitude, methodology or philosophy. Although it is all these things, it does not exist in isolation. It never has. This philosophy, demanding mutual trust and respect, is deeply rooted in the blood-soaked soil of German battlefields and endures as a central tenet of German military leadership that is an organic component of *Bundeswehr* doctrine. Importing any foreign doctrine can be a perilous practice and requires a great deal of thought, preparation, and adjustment; attempting to take a single piece of a greater incorporated whole makes the challenge that much greater. Thus, *Auftragstaktik* cannot be imported as a one-off technique and slipped into our non-German methods, organizations, and practices. It must be part of a greater renewal, an integrated leadership philosophy that gathers the manifold aspects of enlightened leadership together into a holistic command climate. This is not the same as saying it cannot be done. Whether in the military, in medicine, the arts, or in business, learning from what is now referred to as a best practice has always been an excellent way to improve your own understanding of how to improve what your organization does.

But it must be done knowingly and with great care.

Historically, Canadian military doctrine has never been trend-setting or innovative.[1] Having been a former British colony, then a stalwart member of the British Empire and thereafter a member of the British Commonwealth of Nations, for the better part of two centuries Canada was resolutely fixated on military-doctrine it learned from the British. This emulation was not confined solely to tactical doctrine. Canadians understood war and warfare in British terms, and that included how we structured our armed services, how we dressed them, how we administered them and, most importantly, how we led our soldiers, sailors, and aircrews in peace and in war. So proud of our British heritage were we that in the Royal Canadian Navy, many of our officers, whether born on the Prairies or in the Rocky Mountains, affected British accents – so-called 'wardroom accents'. This doctrine fit well since Canadian societal norms and practises were also British. As immigration and world events changed Canadian society, so too did these influences change the Canadian military. In the 1960s and 1970s we gave up British uniforms. In the 1980s and 1990s we abandoned much of the remainder of this mimicry, finally realizing Canadian soldiers, sailors, and aircrews had acquitted themselves with great valour, distinction, and initiative in two world wars, the Korean War, and literally dozens of UN operations around the globe.

As it began a long period of introspection and renewal, the Canadian Armed Forces were faced with the reality that although it sought doctrine that was its own, it had to appreciate that it would surely be a junior partner in any fighting coalitions that would inevitably be commanded by one of the larger NATO allies. In practice, this meant that Canadian military doctrine would have to move closer to the American equivalent if for no other reason than to better understand them and enhance the integration of its forces under their coalition leadership. As Canada was looking inward, so were its allies, and these decades saw some radical upheavals in American, and subsequently NATO, military doctrine.

American journals were filled with new ideas, many of which were misinterpretations or even distortions of German doctrine.

The process began with a fascination with German battlefield effectiveness in the Second World War and quickly moved to *Auftragstaktik;* thereafter shifting to concepts like Mobile Defence, AirLand Battle, Mission Command, the so-called (if mythical) Revolution in Military Affairs, 4th Generation Warfare, NetWar, and eventually the imaginary (and dangerous) Effects Based Operations. All these concepts buffeted first the American military, then NATO and, as a logical consequence, Canada's armed forces.

So, has our collective adoption of *Auftragstaktik* and Mission Command into our diverse national doctrines been successful? No, not really. As someone recently noted, *Auftragstaktik* is the best leadership doctrine that everyone loves but nobody practises. That is perhaps harsh since many military leaders, including me, have espoused and embraced this leadership philosophy. But as US Marine Corps (USMC) BG (Retd) Andrew Milburn recently wrote in an essay in *Small Wars Journal,*[2] the American military has a cultural problem of micromanagement. General Milburn is correct, sadly. And the problem is in no way restricted to the American military; it is a NATO, if not a global, affliction.

What does the history of our adoption of new doctrine tell us? That is a question laden with implications. Allow me to begin with a short aside; it is the story of my own personal journey towards the appreciation of new doctrine. My doctrinal and tactical conversion came relatively late. I had been an army officer for a full decade before I learned how important it was to know everyone's doctrine and not just your own. Where your own doctrine was lacking or weak, you could then strengthen it with ideas from others. In this case, the idea in question was that commanders had to make the enemy their tactical focal point, and I well recall the day in 1986 when I was taught to stop focusing on ground and shift my tactical focus to the enemy.

I had been at the German *FüAk* only a couple months and was still very much wedded to the doctrine that I had studied in my own army's command and staff college two years before. The class was given a quick tactical problem and allotted two hours of individual time to solve it. The solution was to be a graphical overlay order; no written orders, just map symbols on a 1:50,000 scale military map. I was to discover that this was a typically German approach. I had only been introduced to the concept of mission analysis (*Auswertung des Auftrages*) a few days before. I struggled with it, coming up with the mission: **33 Brigade will attack and hold Objective A**. On my map, I chose the dominant piece of terrain where the enemy was expected to be, and I labelled it *Objective A*. I then added some boundaries, put in several intermediate objectives on the way to the main objective and began to calculate my tactical groupings, tasks, time and space.

As I worked on my solution, the course director, an energetic *Panzergrenadier* named *Oberst i.G.* Einar Hermannsen, dropped by and peered over my shoulder. "*Herr Major*," he quietly said, then he switched to English, "why are you attacking a piece of ground? Did not your commander tell you that one of your tasks was to destroy the enemy to the north of you?"

"Yes, *Herr* Oberst," I replied. "But the enemy is dug in on *Objective A* and so I have chosen to attack the objective."

He smiled enigmatically and began to walk me through my logic. He went about this slowly, because he had reverted to his native German, and he wanted to be sure I understood the lesson.

He started by asking me why I was giving my brigade *two* missions. I was puzzled. In the decade that I had been an army officer it had been normal to get missions like *seek and destroy* or *attack and destroy* or *attack and hold*. The first part of *Oberst* Hermannsen's lesson was to make me decide what I wanted the brigade to do to the enemy. Was it to attack?

"Yes," I replied.

"What did your commander tell you to do?"

"Destroy the enemy," I said.

The *Oberst* stared at me blankly and said nothing.

Slowly, I said, "I intend to destroy the enemy by attacking him."

"*Gut!*", smiled the *Oberst*. "But are they the same thing? If you attack and do not destroy the enemy, then have you succeeded or failed?"

"Failed," I said.

"*Nein!* You are mistaken. If you tell a subordinate to attack, and he does it, then the outcome is irrelevant." I felt that the good *Oberst* was splitting hairs; but I was not going to argue with my course director and said nothing. I had only been at the *FüAk* a matter of weeks and I was feeling my neck.

He continued. "You have given two *distinct* missions to your brigade and neither of them relates directly to the mission that you were given by your own commander."

I started to get my legs under me and gently protested. "But, *Herr Oberst*, surely an attack mission implies that I want the enemy destroyed?"

Once again, the sharp and familiar "*Nein!* There are many, many reasons for a commander to attack," he explained. "Your force may be a distraction, a fixing force or part of a larger turning force. In this case, you want the enemy destroyed (*Vernichtet*). In *Bundeswehr* parlance that means that you must reduce the enemy's combat power to below 30% effectiveness. Your commander has ordered you to make the enemy unit combat ineffective," he explained.

I was beginning to see where this lesson was going – or so I thought. "So", I said, "I should change my mission to "destroy and hold"? Again, there was the mute, grim, enigmatic smile.

"Why do you insist on making life complicated for your subordinates?" he asked. Part two of the lesson was about to begin.

The *Oberst* changed tack. "*Herr Major,* why are you focused on the ground? What does you capturing ground have to do with destroying the enemy?"

Now, let me say that the word epiphany is used a lot these days. Used properly, the word should connote a spiritually or religiously significant revelation. Quite honestly, that was how I felt at that moment. Unexpectedly, I saw where the *Oberst* was leading me. My entire life as a tactical officer had been focused on the ground I had to fight on. Naturally, the enemy was considered key and when conducting tactical estimates, the enemy was always considered before all other factors. That was not the same as making the enemy the focus of my tactical thoughts and actions. If I focused on the ground, then the enemy could easily fool me.

What if the enemy left before I got there? Would I still need to attack *Objective A*, a piece of ground now vacant? I suddenly realized how foolish attacking an empty piece of ground would be in the context of his explanation – even though, had this been two years before when I was at my own staff college, such an attack would have been correct. In fact, when I was a student on the Canadian Army's Combat Team Commander's course, we routinely assaulted ground that had been abandoned by the enemy – sometimes we could see them leaving while we attacked! The *Oberst* was teaching me that I had to look up from the ground. I needed to focus on the enemy. That is why the commander had given me the order to *destroy* the enemy.

All the details of this revelation flashed through my mind like lightning. I could see *Oberst* Hermannsen waiting for a reply to his question.

"*Herr Oberst*", I began, "the ground is merely the common medium over which we are fighting. The enemy and I use the same ground so I must stop focusing on it and change my focus to the enemy. If I focus on the enemy and destroy him, then the ground will be mine automatically."

Oberst Hermannsen smiled one more time.

"*Sehr gut, Herr Major. Sehr gut!*" He tapped me lightly on the shoulder and turned to look over the work of one of my German classmates. Before he left, he gently admonished me to think about my love of complex mission statements and intermediate objectives. "We soldiers are simple fellows" he said in German. "Life is already complex; we do not need to make it more so."

The story of my epiphany has much to tell us about the use of language, concepts, and culture. We must begin with basics: What is the purpose of an army? At its heart, every army exists to fight. Naturally, armies do much more than just fight, but an army that cannot fight is not really an army. It belongs on a different scale somewhere between ceremonial guard for tourists and an armed constabulary. The extension of this logic is that when armies fight each other, their aims should be to defeat each other. This seems clear enough. But it is quite nuanced. What constitutes a defeat?

English may well be on its way to becoming humanity's

universal language but sometimes it does not serve us well. When we talk of defeating an enemy, do we mean contain – the act of confining an enemy within a given geographical boundary, thereby removing its freedom of action to employ its combat power? Do we mean disrupt – the act of disturbing the normal command and control so that enemy combat power is less effective? Do we mean neutralize – the act of making enemy's combat power irrelevant? Are you seeing a trend yet? Even if we go to the extent of saying destroy, what do we mean? If an enemy force is reduced by 25%, is it destroyed? What if we get it down to 50%?

This may sound like a numbers game, but it is not. It is all about the rather vague concept of combat power. Whenever we come up against an enemy, we must consider what it is that we need to accomplish. It may be many things, but it is certainly not always destruction. Commanders at all levels need to be clear on their commanders' intent and what outcome is being sought. Luckily, this concept has been part of NATO doctrine long before Mission Command was ever complicated and so this may be a first step towards adapting the tools of *Auftragstaktik* and correctly applying them to achieve the desired outcomes. But there is a long way to go yet.

The 1st century BCE historian Titus Flavius Josephus supposedly wrote that the Romans were sure of victory for their exercises were battles without bloodshed, and their battles were bloody exercises. The adage is well remembered and oft quoted. Unfortunately, Josephus' lesson is even more often ignored. For decades NATO armies have fought unthinking Fantasians, Krasnovians or Granovians to keep tactical fighting skills alive. Whatever their political stripe, these enemies invariably were mechanistic, unimaginative military automatons trapped in a tactical doctrine that allowed very little flexibility or freedom. Originally based on Soviet tactical doctrine, the battle tactics of these generic enemies always made them completely predictable, doctrinally hide-bound, and bloodthirsty to the point of being war criminals. Decades of facing such dull enemies, followed by a decade of fighting a counterinsurgency in Afghanistan, has caused our leaders to become accustomed to beating these deadly but unimaginative foes, thereby lulling us into believing that our own tactical abilities are razor-sharp.

It is much more difficult to fight against a free-thinking adversary. Thus, we establish a rigid command-and-control environment for our enemies so that we can make them predictable. Too often we act as if the enemy has no influence on the timeline. But the enemy gets a vote, and this includes tempo. He is trying to disrupt our tempo just as we are trying to disrupt his, and another story from my *Bundeswehr* days illustrates it well.

While at the *FüAk*, my syndicate went to the British Army Command and General Staff College, (Camberley) to represent a *Bundeswehr* armoured division in a multinational exercise called EX KNIGHT'S CROSS. The British students manned several brigade staffs, a complete mechanized division staff, as well as the corps staff and the enemy force. The US Army Command and General Staff College (Leavenworth) sent a syndicate to represent an American mechanized division. I learned many lessons on this exercise but what impressed me most was that the top two British students played the allied corps commander and the enemy commander respectively. These two students were given a relatively free hand so long as they stayed within broad doctrinal boundaries. The corps commander created a completely traditional defence with the three allied divisions in line abreast. As a believer in what Field Marshal Montgomery called *balance*, the corps commander insisted on battlefield symmetry and alignment – even when it meant giving up ground without fighting. The enemy commander, however, had different ideas. A major in the Royal Artillery, he was highly creative and although he followed Soviet doctrine, he was innovative, decisive, and bold. Within an hour of the opening salvo, he had the allied corps on its back foot and kept a proverbial knife at our throats right up until ENDEX. Ultimately, the enemy was forced to let us win and I remain convinced that had he been allowed, he would have beaten us handily. The Blue Force may have won the exercise but we collectively lost a golden opportunity to learn tactical lessons that would have made us all better commanders.

The best example of what happens when you let the enemy

off the leash was the American joint exercise MILLENNIUM CHALLENGE 2002. USMC MG (Retd) Paul Van Riper, a decorated veteran and ardent trainer was asked to play the role of enemy commander. Joint Forces Command said that new concepts would be tested and validated against an unconstrained enemy force. General Van Riper was so innovative in his attacks that his Red Forces shut down the Blue Forces in one move. The exercise director immediately called ENDEX, reset the exercise, and changed the rules. Van Riper quit and went public with a scathing criticism. Those of us who studied the exercise were disappointed but in no way surprised. We have always said that we wanted realistic innovative training; we just never mean it. Perhaps our leaders should be compelled to read Barbara Tuchman's classic study in bad decisions, *The March of Folly*. It is a wise leader who learns from his mistakes. It is a wiser leader who learns from the mistakes of others.

Commanders at all levels and in all environments need to appreciate that every move they make sends a message to the people they lead. Failure must be an invitation to learn. Naturally, no one likes to fail, especially when your commander is watching. Setting the bar low and then clearing it is a fool's errand and nothing to be proud of. Training to beat a second-class opponent may be comfortable and easily orchestrated but, at best it is a pyrrhic victory. At worst it is a recipe for disaster. Future blood need not be spilled learning lessons, which could be learned now. Field Marshal Erwin Rommel once said that training was the best form of welfare for combat troops: It minimized casualties and kept them alive – but only if it was effective training. A small investment now will pay handsome dividends later. A more realistic and intelligent enemy coupled with more enlightened leadership are two such investments.

Routinely, military leaders come under a lot of criticism. Much of this criticism is not deserved – some is. The old saw that generals are always preparing to fight the last war is not without merit. The past is, after all, a known quantity. It lies solidly within our collective grasp. It is therefore easy to delude ourselves into thinking that looking backward is an appropriate use of history as an instructional model. Beware the incorrect application of historical lessons! The correct use of history would indicate that most of what we learned from yesterday will be nothing more than a basis upon which to build for the future. What this *should* tell us is that we must train to live with uncertainty. We must train our subordinates to do the same and we must trust them so that they can trust us. For without trust there can be no *Auftragstaktik*; for in its most elementary form, *Auftragstaktik* refers to the mutual trust between superiors and subordinates, where superiors set goals, provide resources, and give subordinates free rein to achieve those goals. Recall that this inculcation up and down the chain of command of the idea that commanders were to trust their subordinates and make them, in Professor Bill McAndrew's words, *shareholders of operations* and *not just un-consulted employees*.

The Canadian army, and its NATO partners, have been around this block several times before. Anyone who reads any of the history of the First World War cannot help but become dismayed and frustrated by the seeming rigidity of the Allied High Command and its almost blind insistence on the use of frontal attacks. Of course, we must be careful. Hindsight is invariably unfair to the subject of the investigation. We must be watchful only to look forwards down the arrow of time. We must always try to see what the protagonists saw. In the case of those generals, their training, professional study, and leadership skills did not prepare them to do other than what they did. We can but pity the soldiers who paid in blood so that future leaders could learn. But have we learned from that experience? Remembering the axiom that victorious armies tend to learn less than defeated armies we should be struck by the different lessons learned by opposite sides of the same battles. The French and British, for instance, took completely different lessons from World War I than did the Germans.

The Spanish philosopher and Harvard professor George Santayana warned us almost a century ago that those who refused to learn the lessons of history were doomed to relive its mistakes. With Santayana's admonition on the use of history offering a clear warning to us, do we not risk becoming the object of some future reader's pity? Do we not daily run the risk of being fully ready to fight the *last* war? Can we truly be ready to fight the next war? As dollars (and Euros) become scarcer, does it not make increasing sense to make a more concerted effort to become more professionally proficient? Opportunity is knocking at the door. We have proven time and again that we have the world's most able soldiers; should they not be afforded the world's best leaders?

We began our investigation with insightful comments from my friend and mentor Professor Bill McAndrew and so it is fitting to close this investigation with some of his thoughts that he shared with me[3] some years ago regarding Canadian army doctrine and how it affected its performance in Italy in 1944:

> It was May 1944, the Battle for Rome ... The Germans were fighting a delay battle as they withdrew from their first defensive position, the Gustav Line, to their second, the heavily fortified Hitler Line ... As the 48th [Highlanders] moved through the scrub the right-hand lead company came under fire. They went to ground and began their battle procedure – locate the enemy, engage with fire, gauge his strength, decide if it was a company or battalion objective.
>
> Following doctrine, the Commanding Officer ordered the companies left of the road to stop and keep the line until the situation was cleared. The left company commander then lost radio contact with his two leading platoons. He hollered, the CO's SITREP demands grew louder, and the responses murkier. The company commander had apparently lost control, and hence also the CO. In the meantime, without other orders, the two leading platoons simply kept going to their ultimate objective, a hill overlooking a stream, arriving simultaneously with Germans coming in to occupy their next delaying position. A quick firefight secured the position. Having been outflanked, the other Germans withdrew.
>
> Ironically, a technological breakdown producing a loss of higher control – the touchstones of contemporary doctrine – created conditions for soldiers to exercise initiative and achieve tactical success. Conceivably, they also saved lives. The battalion closed up, having saved half-a day or more in time. The CO regained his composure and recommended a DSO for his lead platoon commander.
>
> Was this an aberration, or typical and representative of the army's tactical doctrine? It's always hazardous to generalize from a single incident – and academics argue endlessly over

how many incidents it takes to make a theory. Battalions displayed remarkable initiative and innovation throughout the war – when given an opportunity...

But, like the Liri Valley action, the question is whether these fit or broke the prevailing doctrinal mould. Above battalion level, doctrine seems to have exerted a dead hand. For Dieppe, staffs produced a 100-page Operation Order that had so much detail a Brigade Commander took his copy ashore because he couldn't memorize it all. When the Germans found this pristine example of micro-management, they called it an 'Aide Memoire for a Map Exercise.' At Agira in Sicily, instead of exploiting a successful but unexpected infiltration, 1st Division withdrew its outflanking force to arrange a deliberate attack on strong points, at considerable cost in lives. At Carpiquet in Normandy, 3rd Division sent a brigade in open formation behind a barrage across an airfield in daylight against well dug-in bunkers. At Coriano in Italy another brigade assaulted down one open slope and up another behind a disappearing barrage that signalled the assault to the defenders. In both results were predictable. In the Rhineland the Canadian Army, with a ration strength of 450,000, prepared the ground with 1200 guns, two tactical air groups, and 1200 bombers. Flooded ground then forced the two assault divisions onto a single main axis where the 3400 available tanks could not deploy. A one-tank front is a one-tank front whether there are two or 2000 behind. Commanders consistently had difficulty applying their strength where and when it was most effective.

These and other instances suggest a doctrinal pattern with several characteristics. Higher headquarters produced detailed plans for lower formations and units to implement. Senior commanders preferred to attack the centre of enemy strength, circles on a map, rather than outflank positions. Doctrine relied on centralized planning; highest level control; staff management of the battlefield; reliance on indirect fire support; scant manoeuvre; cautious exploitation. At least this is how the British Army, in 1944, characterized it.

NOTES

[1] With the possible exception of artillery during the First World War where Canadians invented methodologies and techniques, which are now standard practice in artillery everywhere.

[2] https://smallwarsjournal.com/jrnl/art/losing-small-wars-why-us-military-culture-leads-defeat

[3] Originally told to students and Directing Staff as tactical examples during our battlefield studies in Italy as we walked the ground with veterans and relived the Canadian Army's cracking of the Gothic Line near Rimini. Bill later shared a manuscript with me entitled "Canadian Doctrine – Continuities and Discontinuities".

Kaiser Wilhelm I
Unknown Artist, 1880

CONCLUSIONS

The tactical concept adopted by the German army was "Tactics of Mission or Task [Auftragstaktik] in antithesis to 'Order Style Tactics' [Befehlstaktik] commonly used by other armies. The conceptual and practical difference between these two tactics is fundamental: the first exalts the individual soldier's intelligence and ability, the second tends to mortify them, making them a passive executor of the orders of others.[1]

- Oberst i.G Gerhard Muhm

The great interest in German tactical doctrine displayed by almost every country in the NATO Alliance in the past few decades has had a considerable impact upon the member nations of the Alliance. Impelled by both Britain and America, NATO has officially adopted what has come to be known as a 'manoeuvrist approach' to warfare. One of the pillars of this ill-named manoeuvrist approach was what the new doctrine manuals called Mission Command. Both terms stemming from William Lind's *Maneuver Warfare Handbook*. This view of warfare was not new; it was only new to the majority of NATO. What the British and Americans dubbed a new style of warfare, the Germans considered business as usual for most of the previous two centuries.

Clearly, wherever the terms came from, the tenets of the manoeuvrist approach stem from the Prusso-German school of warfare. German tactical terminology and phraseology now litter many doctrine manuals. American, British, Dutch, and Canadian officers commonly use words like *Schwerpunkt*, *Aufrollen* and *Auftragstaktik*. The paragraph in military orders that used to describe an upcoming operation is now called the Scheme of Manoeuvre, which is actually just a description of the plan – even when no manoeuvre is involved.. This lip service is almost Orwellian in its doublespeak. It gives the impression that the leaders have a manoeuvrist approach. Such language is fraught with intellectual peril and reached its apogee in the ill-fated doctrine of Effects Based Operations. The blithe use of these words disguises a shallow and too often flawed understanding of their meanings and masks the little regard that most officers have of the tactical heritage or historical pedigree of these German terms. Lifting words from another culture and using them without appreciating their historical and conceptual roots de-links the words from their meanings. This problem is further exacerbated when the vocabulary is translated and incorporated into multinational doctrine without any linkages to original meanings. These German words and concepts are idiomatic expressions of a combination of history, culture, and experience. One might reasonably ask whether even the *Bundeswehr*, considering its post-Second World War experience, could rightly claim these concepts. The question becomes even more interesting when one considers whether these concepts are transferable into armies that share practically none of the *Bundeswehr's* social, cultural, or military past.

If the *Bundeswehr* is indeed the tactical heir to the battlefield excellence of the Prussian army, then arguably, current German tactics could be used to improve the future battlefield performance of NATO armies. As a fully integrated military partner, the *Bundeswehr* could teach the rest of the Alliance the fundamentals of its tactical proficiency. At least, so flows the logic. Based on this premise, the US Army, followed closely by the British Army, proceeded to rewrite its battlefield doctrine using the hybrid invention of Maneuver Warfare, with its strong reliance on the Prusso-German school, as the new foundation for its future tactics. Unfortunately, in the rush to adopt ideas like *Auftragstaktik*, doctrine writers and senior military leaders alike largely disregarded the historical and cultural roots of this leadership philosophy. Instead, *Auftragstaktik* was bolted onto an existing *Befehlstaktik* doctrine thereby creating irreconcilable contradictions. It is unthinkable that anyone would seriously suggest that NATO partners should adopt *Bushido*, the ancient cult of the Japanese *Samurai*, as a leadership culture. Such a suggestion would surely be seen as laughable. The obvious cultural and historical roots of the Japanese warrior culture are foreign to us. Yet, this has not been seen as an obstacle with the introduction of *Auftragstaktik*. Despite its foreign cultural components, NATO armies have gone ahead and adopted this idea. Translating *Auftragstaktik* into Mission Command has made it easier to pronounce, but it has not made it any less foreign. Consequently, there can be little hope of this conceptual graft taking hold. Unless the non-German armies that wish to incorporate *Auftragstaktik* gain a better understanding of the cultural, social, and structural changes that led to the development of this tool, eventual failure is inevitable.

✠ ✠ ✠

The French Revolution shattered the old monarchical order and introduced new warfighting concepts to Europe. Napoleon did far more than simply attempt to conquer Europe; he changed the military paradigm in existence before his arrival. The Prussian army was particularly slow to adapt, and so fell victim to the battlefield prowess of the new French armies. As a direct result of the defeat at Jena, Prussia began a fundamental transformation of her army. The change was both a structural and a conceptual renewal. Scharnhorst revitalized the Prussian staff structure and created the General Staff. Gneisenau infused the army with a new conceptual life by the introduction of his concept of leadership by directives. Clausewitz provided a new interpretation of Napoleon and, thereby, redefined the very nature of battle. These three men, as leaders amongst a particularly dedicated group of reformers, rebuilt the Prussian army after the disaster of Jena and, in the process, created a new school of warfare. The proponents of this new Prussian School went on to reshape the Prussian army using the ideas of these men. The General Staff became the principal intellectual governing force of the army. It carefully selected and then rigorously educated only the best and most talented young officers in the art and science of war and consequently, by the middle of the 19th century, the Staff's systematic selection and careful grooming had developed sufficiently to produce *institutionalized excellence*.

The great strength of *Auftragstaktik* was its interconnectivity with other facets of Prussian warfighting. This leadership philosophy could not work in isolation. *Auftragstaktik* was not simply a case of having commanders give subordinates instructions and then expect them to achieve success. By its nature, *Auftragstaktik* required several fundamental preconditions, without which the experiment in balancing discipline and independent thought would not work. Like the Clausewitzian model of war, *Auftragstaktik* was a complicated mixture of contradictions. Discipline demanded rigid obedience to orders, yet orders *had* to be disobeyed if the situation at lower levels made them irrelevant. All the pieces of this complex leadership philosophy needed to work in unison, or the mechanism would fail.

First and foremost among the required prerequisites was trust. Trust was a manifestation of mutual respect among soldiers. The army was an honourable profession, a *Brüderschaft*, a brotherhood. Soldiers of all ranks shared a common *Korpsgeist*; they felt that they belonged to an important cultural group.[2] Prussian soldiers were respected, not only within the army, but also within the greater German society. They all wore the king's coat. This trust was not only directed upward, but more importantly, it was directed *downward*, from officers to soldiers. The idea of shared responsibility, which was initially so well demonstrated between Gneisenau and Blücher, slowly spread throughout the army. All soldiers were made to feel that they were stakeholders in the successful accomplishment of their commanders' missions. Over time, Prussian soldiers grew to appreciate that it was not only their right and privilege to act in a manner that would ensure success; it was their duty. Critically, if this duty meant that they were to disobey irrelevant orders, then they were not only allowed to do so, but were also *obliged* to do so.

Second; there had to be a commonly held perception of the nature of battle. The Clausewitzian maelstrom of chaos, friction, and disorder, was this common perception. Nevertheless, this alone was not enough, for the understanding that war was chaos was but one half of the equation. The other half was what this understanding meant to soldiers in combat; they had to think for themselves. Thus, the Clausewitzian view of battle merged with the Napoleonic principal of freedom of action. This principle of freedom, as expressed by Gneisenau's control by directives, gave every Prussian soldier the understanding that he needed to act independently *within* the chaos of battle, even to the extent of creating more chaos. Clearly, Scharnhorst's "phlegmatic" Germans had become transformed. Moreover, the imposition of order upon chaos by superior commanders, as anathema to the Clausewitzian model, was avoided. This gave all soldiers the freedom of action necessary to make decisions based upon their local circumstances, guided only by their own judgement and their commanders' intent. Although there may not have been any need to disregard orders, knowing that they could, if necessary, lent great psychological impetus to the pursuit of tactical success. This freedom to act strengthened the mutual trust between leader and subordinate and lent dignity to the ability of the individual soldier; it "exalted the intelligence and capabilities of the individual soldier."[3] The marriage of the Clausewitzian model of war with the Gneisenaun dictum of acting in accordance with a commander's intent formed an intellectual framework unlike any that existed in other armies. This framework breathed life into *Auftragstaktik*.

Third, a guiding organization was a requisite precondition. There had to be someone in control, someone that could monitor and guide the growth and implementation of the new intellectual concepts within the army. Of necessity, this control had to outlive any one individual, and so it fell to an organization. The Prussian General Staff provided this guidance. By creating a body of men committed not only to military success but, more importantly, to the pursuit of intellectual and professional excellence, the Prussian army established a uniquely useful organization. Specially chosen and rigorously trained, these men became the embodiment of Prussian military excellence. So successful were they, that the Prussian General Staff became the enduring model for all other armies to copy well into the present century. From Scharnhorst's early restructuring of the *Quartiermeisterstab*, his followers continued to build upon his well-laid foundations. The creation of a special school, the *Kriegsakademie*; the seeding of General Staff officers throughout the army and other government organizations;

the establishment of direct and parallel chain of command to the Chief of the General Staff; and the Chief of General Staff's direct access to the king, all contributed to the general improvement of the army.

There is the immense personal contribution made by Helmuth von Moltke. Moltke was the paragon of a Prussian General Staff officer. This quiet and intellectual officer brought many of the great reforms begun half a century before him to their culmination. His reorganization of the General Staff and his strong adherence to Gneisenau's control by directives raised the professional competence, as well as the professional reputation of the Prussian army to new heights. His long tenure and his personal dedication to the principles of *Auftragstaktik* virtually guaranteed that this concept would outlive him. Although singular in his contribution to Prussian and German military thinking, Moltke was by no means unique. The General Staff, as the guardians of the Prussian military art, produced several generations of fine military thinkers and leaders by the time Moltke came to prominence. There was an unbroken intellectual chain from Scharnhorst to Moltke. It is indicative of the collective intellectual unity of the General Staff that another General Staff officer, and sometime rival of Moltke, could demonstrate one of the most often quoted examples of *Auftragstaktik*. During the Franco Prussian War, General Edwin von Manteuffel, commander of the Southern Army, gave direction to his generals: "I herewith ratify in advance all measures, for which my sanction is necessary, so that the hands of the commanding generals may not be tied by any regulations." No better example could illustrate the effects of over half a century of intellectual and structural development. In contrast, Charles de Freycinet, French Minister of War, demanded that all military decisions be submitted to him personally, and that military commanders could make decisions only in the case of extreme emergency.[4]

Thus, the complicated interactions required to enable the complex leadership concept of *Auftragstaktik* to flourish worked in concert. Trust formed the basis of the relationship between officers and their soldiers. Soldiers everywhere felt themselves to be part of a special community, a brotherhood. There was a shared understanding of the nature of war, and there was a large, professionally competent governing body that regulated all these complex interactions. Victory in war was not left to chance; it was studied as an art and a science. The military became a profession.

The lasting lesson, however, remains one that is easily overlooked. *Auftragstaktik* did not spring fully formed from the mind of Helmuth von Moltke. Nor was this uniquely German military concept a recent innovation. It had been born of dire necessity and its early development had been a slow and not always smooth process. In the half century between the Reform Commission and the arrival of Moltke as the Chief of the Great General Staff, the Prussian army had undergone fundamental change and continuous development. *Auftragstaktik* was the product of this change and development and, even during the time of Moltke, the product was imperfectly formed. It would require another half century of development, sometimes in the laboratory of war, before *Auftragstaktik* would be an integral intellectual part of the German military culture. The warning to other armies should therefore be obvious: Lest they are willing to undergo the types of reforms experienced by the Prussian and later by German armies, there is little chance of other armies being able to make significant use of *Auftragstaktik*.

NOTES

[1] Gerhard Muhm, "*La tattica tedesca nella campagna d'Italia*". This quote was the topic of many conversations between me and *Oberst* Muhm over the course of several years. Specifically, the text is from a monograph written by the *Oberst* and given to me during one of our many meetings.

[2] Interestingly, current German General Staff officers often display this *Korpsgeist* in unique ways. In German, there is a form of the language commonly referred to in the army, as *Generalstabsdeutsch*. This refers to the fact that General Staff officers make heavy use of the genitive case, a complex grammatical case that is all but lost in normal conversational German. At the *FüAk* we were frequently corrected when using slang or low-level German, reminded that General Staff officers did not speak *Truppendeutsch*.

[3] Muhm.

[4] Howard, *The Franco-Prussian War*, (London, 1962), p. 418.

General Gerhard David Graf von Scharnhorst
Portrait by Friederich Bury c. 1820

EPILOGUE - SCHARNHORST'S HEIRS

He who has not fought the Germans does not know war.
- **British Military Aphorism**

wice during a single lifetime, Germany's Great General Staff was at least in part responsible for war on a continental scale.[1] First in 1919 and again in 1945, the victorious Allied Powers, fearing a resurgence of German militarism, outlawed this venerable organization. It was a completely understandable reaction, even if based upon a flawed understanding of the General Staff's function. Today, although still formally outlawed, *Bundeswehr* officers who are graduates of the two-year *Führungsakademie* command and staff course[2], including me, proudly use the postnominal *i.G.* (*im Gerenalstabsdienst*) – in the service of the General Staff. These coveted postnominals may only be used by *FüAk* graduates. But you may wonder, if there is no General Staff, how does this make sense? How can someone be in the service of a non-existent organization?

To better understand this Teutonic intellectual gymnastic, we must ask ourselves if the modern *Bundeswehr* is the rightful heir to the ancient military traditions of German battlefield excellence or if there has been an historical schism (see Chapter 5) brought on by the 1933 Nazi takeover, the 1945 surrender, and the subsequent 1956 re-establishment of the German military. Some German historians have facetiously argued that the *Bundeswehr* is burdened with 'too much history'. What has all this history meant to the current *Bundeswehr* – especially considering the political climate of modern Europe?

The changing map of Europe in the 1990s caused many to again view Germany with a concern not experienced for several generations. The break-up of the Balkans following so closely upon the heels of German re-unification renewed fears of renascent German militarism. Twice already in the 20th century, Germany had initiated firestorms which engulfed entire continents. Did Europeans yet again need to fear the professional skills of the *Bundeswehr*? More recently, as some European countries appeared to lurch towards right-wing strongmen to lead them, the question arose again and, arguably, remains unanswered.

The title subject goes to the heart of the German civil-military relationship, but even more fundamental is the question of the professional competence of the *Bundeswehr*. Has Germany's military managed to successfully reach back through its chequered past and retrieve the good of Scharnhorst and Gneisenau without being tainted by the 20th century insanity of Kaiser Wilhelm II or worse, the evil of Nazism? Is the modern *Bundeswehr* the military heir to the battlefield glories of Frederician Prussia or Wilhelmine Germany? Does it legitimately wear the mantle of military excellence for which Scharnhorst laid the foundation?

To answer these questions, it is necessary to briefly review the history of the German army for it is impossible to understand the modern German military without having an appreciation of its strong Prussian tradition. As we have seen in the foregoing chapters, the long and steady developments, which created the superb fighting organizations and masterful feats of German arms, were not accomplished painlessly. The evolution of some of the world's best battlefield doctrine occurred because of a long and constant struggle. Like the country itself, the German army was forged in the furnace of conflict over many generations.

Through wars and political upheaval, German soldiery withstood many tests but perhaps none so intrinsically demanding as the 1955 creation of the *Bundeswehr*. No war was as devastating to any army as was the Second World War to the *Reichswehr*. The rebuilding of a professional military after the gangrene of Nazism meant the bridging of a chasm in terms of tradition, professional skills, ethos, doctrine, and most importantly civil-military relations. One cannot but wonder whether the founders of the *Bundeswehr* were successfully able to bridge this gap.

The halcyon days of the German military tradition recall Gerhard von Scharnhorst, Carl von Clausewitz, August von Gneisenau, and Helmuth von Moltke. In the nearly two centuries separating the reforms of Scharnhorst and national re-unification, the German military endured the full range of military experience from the dizzying heights of total battlefield success to the crushing depths of absolute annihilation. Is it possible that any organization that lived through such change could recapture the qualities of professional competence created during its golden age? The answer is inextricably bound to how the *Bundeswehr* came to be re-established.

Although a fascinating study, the details of the formation of the *Bundeswehr* per se is not the issue. More important, through all its iterations, the army had been seen by many as the soul of the nation. For generations the army was the anchor of the ship of state. Most of the population saw it in a positive light. Frederick the Great had created the army as the school of the nation and in turn the army had helped to forge the German empire with, in Bismarck's phrase, 'blood and iron'. Unlike most armies though, the German army did not follow a linear path in its evolution from the 18th to the 20th century. The path had been, in many ways, a national *via dolorosa* beset with political and social problems which were not to play themselves out fully until the wars of the 20th century.

For reasons unique to Germany the army had always bound itself inextricably to the national political leadership. As we have seen, the Prusso-German military tradition was unique in Europe and an important part of that uniqueness – from Frederick the Great to the ignominious Adolf Hitler and through all the intervening national leaders – was that the army had always held an intimate relationship with the head of state. The price the army paid for this relationship was always high and ultimately led to its own destruction.

On at least four occasions the army had to re-establish itself. Inevitably this was as a direct result of some cataclysmic political event. The first restructuring came after Napoleon Bonaparte's 1807 victory at Jena and Auerstädt, where upon the army was fundamentally reformed and rebuilt by Scharnhorst. The changes were manifold and profound and led to a tactical proficiency unequalled in Europe. The second reform came after the defeat in the First World War, the abdication of the Kaiser and the subsequent declaration of a republic. General Hans von Seeckt was forced to restructure the *Reichswehr* in accordance with the punitive Treaty of Versailles. Von Seeckt's genius created the cadre for future expansion while systematically embedding the excellence of the past into a 100,000-man structure. The third incarnation came in 1935 at the hands of the Nazis with the creation of the *Wehrmacht*. As it had traditionally done, the army bound itself to the national leadership. Arguably, without the complicity of many senior officers the *Wehrmacht* could not have perverted the battlefield excellence of the German army, but that remains a moot point. The fourth and most recent rebirth of the German army came approximately a decade after the Second World War, and it is this last incarnation which interests us most.

This last effort was the product of the intensive work of a small group of ex-*Wehrmacht* officers who under the watchful guidance of the Allied Powers, re-introduced the army (*Heer*), and later the navy (*Marine*) and air force (*Luftwaffe*), into German society. The dilemmas facing these men was fundamentally different than those faced by their predecessors. The founders of the new German army (*Bundeswehr*) could not turn easily to past practices, traditions, and structures for their new model army. Many of the practices of the past were indelibly stained by the scourge of Nazism and could not therefore be rehabilitated. They could not simply resurrect the *Wehrmacht* with its disastrous mistakes; yet neither could they abandon their national history.

In 1950, coincident with the Korean War, Britain and America began secretly to call for a German contribution to the growing costs of European defence. German Chancellor Konrad Adenauer, himself targeted by the Nazi regime for 'transport', established a small and secret group to work on the problem of how to rearm Germany. Five years later, on 12 November 1955 in a small but important ceremony, 101 German volunteers swore to uphold the constitution of the federal republic and to defend the German nation against all enemies.

The date chosen for the rebirth of the German Armed Forces, chosen by Theodor Blank, the first defence minister, was no accident. It was a significant day for those who knew anything of Germany's military past; It was the 200th birthday of Scharnhorst, the man who in 1807 had begun the reform of the Prussian army after the disastrous defeat at Jena. The unspoken message, undoubtedly lost on most, was clear to the astute observer. The new armed forces were to be guided by the positive influences of the distant past. As the father of both military reform and the General Staff, Scharnhorst's spirit was to guide the new *Bundeswehr*. The near past was to be buried and with that burial Germany was to return to her honourable traditions which had first built a nation and thereafter an empire.

Was it possible? Could one look back through history and skip over those distasteful portions and select only those positive traditions. The founders of the *Bundeswehr* believed they could. They were convinced that they were starting with a *tabula rasa*, a clean slate, and that they could therefore write their own script, one which ignored their Nazi past. They set about to do just that.

As one might imagine, this was no simple task. Armies, like dogs and racehorses, have pedigrees. As Albrecht Dürer reminded us, they are also invariably products of the societies which create them. Had the *Bundeswehr* adopted the trappings of modern armies only to be, at its heart, the same army that had almost brought western civilization to its knees? Or was it possible that the army, which swept to victory in 1815, 1848, 1860, and 1871, could be revived? Rather than look at the superficial aspects of the army, with its modern equipment, American influenced structure, and English-speaking leadership, one must focus on the conceptual aspects of the *Bundeswehr*. Perhaps it would be better to ask whether the pedigree had been corrupted? Are the concepts of leadership and discipline the same as they were in the

19th century? Has the doctrine changed significantly? What is the internal structure of the *Bundeswehr*? The leadership may speak English and contribute to the leadership of NATO, but what are their fundamental beliefs, and how do they compare to their fathers' and grandfathers' virtues and values?

The reality of the modern *Bundeswehr* is that there is a continuous and unbroken intellectual train of thought from Scharnhorst to the present day. This is true despite the twelve-year Nazi *interregnum* as well as the army's disbandment for over a decade. There are several important reasons why this is so. First, German culture is deeply rooted in its own past. Few cultures so firmly embrace their past as does the German. Tradition is a powerful prime mover in the social fabric of the society. This is both cultural and sociological. Second, unlike pluralistic North American cultures, Germany is still exceptionally homogeneous ethnically, linguistically, and in terms of Christian beliefs. Third, there is a certain pragmatism in the German national character which does not allow the easy discard of any successful tool. One does not have to live in Germany very long to discover that the old virtues of hard work, frugality, and continuity run daily life. There is a common German expression which reminds everyone that *Ordnung ist ein halb des Lebens* (good order is half of life). These factors combine in all aspects of German daily life, from the mundane to the sublime. For instance, chimney sweeps all over the country still wear black leather clothing and top hats and repairmen invariably wear blue overalls. There is still a strict law governing what is an allowable German name for the christening of a child. It would be illogical and inconsistent to believe that the army would be any different from its parent society. Good doctrine and strong tactical concepts would not be discarded with the changing of the guard. They remained as valid in 1955 as they did in the age of Moltke.

When the *Wehrmacht* was resuscitated as the *Bundeswehr* in 1955, the Adenauer government was most careful in choosing which officers would be allowed to return to the reborn institution. Mistakes had been made before and could not be made again. A strong democratic tradition was taking root in West Germany and the same had to be true of the *Bundeswehr*. Consequently, the basic model that the army was founded upon was one heavily influenced by the occupying American army's democratic tradition. Further, in order that previous mistakes would not be repeated, the officers designing the new force instituted several concepts which were necessarily foreign to the German military tradition. Contrary to what the anti-democratic Prussian minister of defence, General Gustav von Griesheim, had stated, the military was *not* to be built as an island separated from society. Unlike before, soldiers were not to be a separate caste without the political rights of normal citizens. Thus, in stark contrast with their longstanding historical tradition, *Bundeswehr* soldiers were to be conscripted but without abrogating their rights of citizenship. They were not just soldiers. Rather, they were *Staatsbürger in Uniform* (citizens in uniform).

Another concept dubbed *Innere Führung*[3] was made a central theme in the education and training of all uniformed personnel irrespective of rank or background. The *Zentrum für Innere Führung* was established and charged with ensuring that everyone in uniform established and maintained an inner moral compass. Having spent a week at the *Zentrum*, I can attest to the seriousness with which the *Bundeswehr* taught the issues of morality, and of the virtues and duties of citizenship. These and other subtler differences were to act as checks and balances against the recurrence of past abuses of power.

> **I swear to loyally serve the Federal Republic of Germany and to courageously defend the rights and the liberty of the German people, so help me God.**
> *Ceremonial Oath Sworn by Bundeswehr Officers and NCOs*

Nonetheless, all these newly introduced checks and balances were not enough. The greatest single tool of past German battlefield victories had to be addressed. The prime mover of the success enjoyed by the German army throughout the 18th, 19th, and 20th-centuries was the strong central control exerted by the Great

131

General Staff. From its inception, the General Staff had set the course for all major developments in the army (and later in the navy [*Admiralstab*] and the air force [*Generalstab der Luftwaffe*]). In Trevor Dupuy's words, the most significant result of the general staff system was the 'institutionalization of excellence'. By design, the brightest young officers were hand-picked and trained for the most critical positions of leadership. It is not surprising then that this very institution had twice become the target of Germany's victorious enemies.

Whether the work of the *Zentrum* will have a lasting effect remains to be seen, but an incident, which occurred during my time as a student at the *FüAk* makes me believe that progress is being made. One of the subjects that we studied during our two-year course was artillery fire-planning. On several occasions we gathered in plenary session (without the French army students who were not integrated into the military side of NATO at that time) for top secret briefings. During one such briefing, the subject of nuclear weapons was broached and the colonel giving the briefing displayed a highly classified map of probable targets should nuclear release be authorized. Interestingly, as well as targets in Poland, Czechoslovakia and other Warsaw Pact countries, there were targets in East Germany. Some of the German students began to stir in their seats. The colonel asked for quiet so that he could continue. One of my classmates, a captain, stood and interrupted the colonel. In a few sharp sentences, the captain politely but firmly explained that what they were doing was a criminal act, one which violated his sworn oath as an officer and asked the colonel to cease. The colonel, taken aback by such a blatant accusation told the captain to please retake his seat. Half a dozen other German captains stood. One of them reminded the colonel that their oath was sworn *not only* to the *Bundesrepublik* but to *des deutschen Volkes*. Planning a nuclear attack on the people they swore to defend was unthinkable and the standing officers turned and left the classroom. The embarrassed colonel summarily dismissed the class.

Although the General Staff was outlawed, von Seeckt saw it as the very heart and soul of the army and so it was secretly reincarnated as the Army Office and lived on. Outlawed yet again after Second World War, the founders of the *Bundeswehr* could not imagine an army or armed forces without a strong central staff, but how to take the best of this system and leave out the worst? *Innere Führung* would surely solve that dilemma. There could be no General Staff – even by another name. The solution was at once clever and curious. There could be no General Staff but there could be a group of officers especially selected and rigorously trained to serve on the General Staff were it ever allowed to return. Thus, the concept of *im Generalstabsdienst (i.G.)* – literally in the service of the General Staff, was born. Through this interesting Teutonic quirk, which allowed officers to be in the service of a non-existent organization, the *Bundeswehr* in effect re-established the Great General Staff. They brought it back in all but name for all three services. In the army, it is now called the Army Office – shades of von Seeckt!

Having successfully breathed new life into the General Staff, even if it was only a select group of officers who put the letters *i.G.* after their names, all that remained was to re-forge the link with Germany's military past. All armed forces have need of staff colleges to train their officers. The *Bundeswehr* was no different. The old *Kriegsakademie*, renamed as *die Führungsakademie der Bundeswehr* was established in Hamburg. Here, the *Bundeswehr* broke with the American model, preferring to re-establish its old training philosophy. They saw the need to recreate what had been called the *Selekta*, the elite.

Unlike most modern armed forces, the great majority of German officers are not given extensive command and staff training. For instance, in the Canadian, American, or British forces, approximately half of all officers receive staff training. The German model is fundamentally different in that entrance to the staff college is by rigorous competition and examination, and the payoff is commensurate with the effort. In the *Bundeswehr*, graduates of the *FüAk* are guaranteed to become colonels – even though they are selected to attend the college as captains. The pyramidal structure found in most armies exists in the *Bundeswehr* in terms of rank but, unlike most, only those officers at the very top receive the intensive schooling required of General Staff officers. The *Bundeswehr* trains only the top ten to fifteen percent of its officers to allow them to advance to the highest level. Very few officers make it to the two-year command and staff course. Only *i.G.* officers can rise to be Inspector General of the Army, Chief of Staff, or Inspector General of the Armed Forces. Although only a small percentage of the officer population at large, *i.G.* officers form over ninety percent of all generals. Officers who are *i.G.* control the armed forces, just as in days of old.

The creation of these *i.G.* officers has re-established the General Staff with few of the negative and archaic traditions and strictures, and this process has had a positive effect upon the *Bundeswehr* as a whole. The young officers of all three services who are selected to go to Hamburg are schooled in the old traditions of selfless work, tactical brilliance, and military efficiency. They, unlike their NATO brethren, are forced to abandon any regimental or branch affiliation. Upon entrance to the *FüAk,* their affiliation and loyalty pivots away from their previous branches to the *Bundeswehr as a whole body.* By this process, there is an unbroken line of thought from Scharnhorst to any graduate of today's *FüAk.* Despite the passage of two centuries, and discounting the technological leaps, there is no doubt that today's young graduate would be comfortable talking to his predecessors as peers in terms of tactics, understanding of shared concepts of battle and the fundamentals of battlefield command. The German *i.G.* officer of today is easily a match of his historical Great General Staff predecessors.

✠ ✠ ✠

The German army has seen many changes over the course of its long and oft-chequered history. Taking the accession of Frederick the Great as our starting point, the nearly three centuries have seen German soldiery both idealized as the epitome of military skill as well as demonstrating the shocking depths to which an army can sink. Throughout its corporate life the German army, and by extension the armed forces, has somehow managed to maintain its *Korpsgeist* or *esprit de corps*. This resilience has been nothing short of remarkable. Even more remarkable has been the strength of continuity in terms of dedication to excellence, tactical thought, and command philosophy. Arguably, no other army has been able to maintain its focus as has the German army. From Scharnhorst through to any recent graduate of the *FüAk*, the bedrock of the army has been the intellectual leadership provided by the General Staff. Through its institutional excellence, this body of officers has provided the basis for expansion in times of need and has been its cadre – its intellectual seed corn – in times of retrenchment. Consequently, the iron will of Scharnhorst, the intellect of Clausewitz, and the brilliance of Moltke live on in today's *Bundeswehr*.

NOTES

[1] The following observations are derived from my personal experiences with the *Bundeswehr* in the two years during which I was a student at the *FüAk*. I lived in Germany for seven years and having learned to read, write, and speak the language I worked diligently to try to understand my new friends and colleagues. Two academic works were of value in helping to frame my own experiences in an historical perspective for the purposes of this chapter: *The Goose Step is Verboten: The German Army Today* by Eric Waldman and *Reforging the Iron Cross* by Donald Abenheim. Both were useful in helping me appreciate how the *Bundeswehr* overcame its Nazi legacy to become an effective instrument of German democracy as well as a loyal and leading NATO partner.

[2] The *FüAk* conducts two staff courses. The senior course is two years long and open to NATO members. There is a nine-month course purely for foreign non-NATO officers. No Germans attend this latter course.

[3] This term has suffered under the burden of translation. It has been translated as inner guidance, moral leadership, ethical training, and various other terms. The term is less important than the concept. All *Bundeswehr* members are given regular training, which is supposed to reset their inner moral compasses and thereby not allow them to fall prey to the temptations of subverting moral and ethical democratic values 'for the good of the service' as did their fathers and grandfathers.

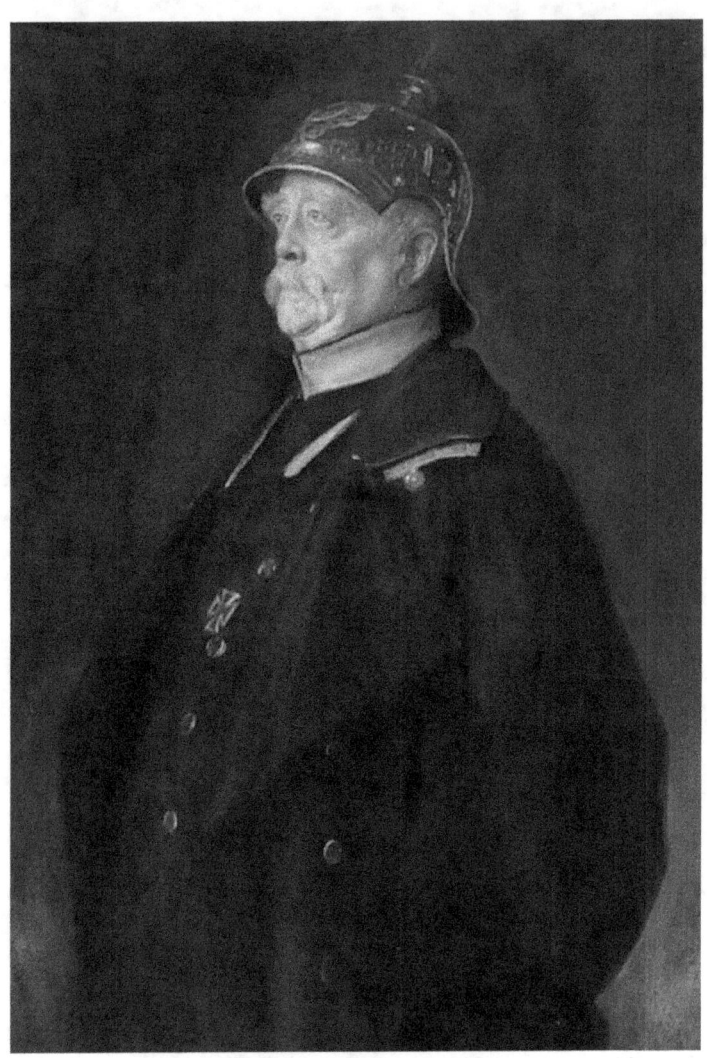

Prinz Otto von Bismarck
Oil by Franz von Lenbach 1884

AFTERWORD

The great questions of our time will not be settled by resolutions and by majority votes – that was the mistake of 1848 and 1849 – but by blood and iron!

- Prinz Otto von Bismarck

A nation's military is an organ of the state and, as we have seen in the case of Prussia, if it is not controlled by the state, then there is a serious risk that the military will use its central position and power within the state to gain undue influence. Ancient Rome's Praetorian Guard was such a military organization; the German General Staff, after 1890, was another. German militarism has become almost a truism. Germans love war and they are good at it – or at least so the public perception seems to be. In fact, we used to have a joke among the foreign students at the *FüAk* that we had played the Germans at their national sport and beaten them – twice! Of course, this is nonsense but even nonsense often has a hint of factual basis. In his *Commentaries on the Gallic Wars*, Julius Caesar praised the German Alemanni tribes' fighting abilities, but he did the same for the Gauls. Let us not forget that both were subdued by the Roman Legions.

Gerhard Ritter's masterful four volume history of German Militarism, *The Sword and the Scepter, The Problem of Militarism in Germany* remains the touchstone text on the subject and there is no need to re-argue here what he has already done so well. Where and when German militarism began is much less important than where it ended. Put another way, the period covered in this investigation can be seen as a prologue to the horrors of two world wars and the deaths of millions of innocent people.

To appreciate the German militarism of the 20th century, we must look beyond the history I have recounted in this book for it really begins with the Moltke the Elder and his misguided break with his teacher's most famous maxim, that war is a political act and as such, in war, politics must have primacy. Moltke turned that idea on its head insisting that once declared war was the purview of the military chain of command and that political considerations should be set aside until victory was achieved. He forgot what Clausewitz had taught him, that war has its own grammar but not its own logic. In other words, the underlying reason for war is always political, even if the fighting is done in ways that ostensibly have little or nothing to do with politics. This reversal of Clausewitz's logic led Prussia, and thereafter Germany, towards the doctrine of 'absolute war', a doctrine which refused political interference once war was engaged. The ultimate effect of this break with Clausewitz's theory cannot be overstated. Individuals like Alfred von Schlieffen, and Erich Ludendorff took this malign doctrine to its ultimate limits, ruinously leading Germany into two cataclysmic world wars which decimated Europe and almost destroyed Germany.

In contrast to Moltke, Otto von Bismarck, first chancellor of modern Germany, although a failed soldier, was the consummate practitioner of *Realpolitik*. In his own words, politics was the art of the possible and he was keenly aware that the new German Reich, sitting in the centre of Europe, had to be ever vigilant that its military gains not be made at the expense of political gains. In other words, Germany had to be conscious of the political consequences of using its military power. These two opposing philosophies brought the two great men into near-continuous conflict. Contrary to Bismarck's opinion of him, Moltke was well-versed in politics. But his misinterpretation of Clausewitz's dictum convinced him that the army could not accept political interference until victory was declared. Conversely, Schlieffen's plan, which disregarded the political consequences of violating Belgian neutrality, ignited the First World War.

Bismarck was the architect of the modern German state and

acted as the midwife to the birth of the Reich in 1871. However, this new military and political entity in the heart of Europe severely disrupted a centuries-old equilibrium of power. Bismarck understood this well and was thus intent on carefully integrating the new Reich into the European framework of political checks and balances. Battlefield brilliance would not be enough. He understood that this integration could succeed only if Germany did not become intoxicated with its new power and pursue a policy of enlargement. He knew that if Germany harboured any visions of expansion, it would inevitably come into conflict with its neighbours. He thus had always appreciated that, as chancellor, it was his great task to reconcile a newly unified Germany with her opponents as soon as possible and hence to establish peaceful relations. He respected Machiavelli's dictum that political power is a zero-sum game that, in any given closed political ecosystem, a country's increased influence could only be achieved at the expense of others in that ecosystem.

Kurfürst Friedrich Wilhelm of Brandenburg, 'The Great Elector'

Oil on canvas Frans Luycx, 1651

ANNEX A: HOHENZOLLERN MONARCHS

Note: Identifying the various rulers of Brandenburg-Prussia-Germany can easily become an exercise in both pedantry and confusion as the rulers had titles that were not consistent across all their holdings. For instance, in 1688, Frederick III became Elector of Brandenburg but on 18 January 1701 was granted the title of King in Prussia (as opposed to King of Prussia), thereby making him Frederick I. The list below is therefore simplified for clarity.

Elector Johann Sigismund (1608 - 1619)
Born in Halle an der Saale 8 November 1572. Died 23 December 1619 in Berlin. He acquired Cleves, Mark, and Ravensburg. He had eight children, three of whom died in infancy.

Elector George Wilhelm I (1619 - 1640)
Born in Cölln (near Berlin) 13 November 1595. Died in Königsberg 1 December 1640. A vassal of the King of Poland and brother-in-law of Gustavus Adolphus. He was a weak and mostly ineffectual ruler. The margravate was almost destroyed under him due to his weakness and vacillation during the Thirty Years' War.

Elector Frederick Wilhelm I (1640 - 1688)
Born in Potsdam 16 February 1620. Died 29 April 1688 in Berlin. He rebuilt the ruined realm and was so admired that even during his lifetime he was dubbed The Great Elector (*der Große Kurfürst*). He was a staunch pillar of the Protestant Church, promoted trade and supported the growing commercial classes. He raised an army of 45,000 shortly after ascending to power and was also a popular social

reformer. In effect, the growth of power of the Hohenzollern dynasty begins with him.

Frederick I of Prussia (1688 - 1713)
Born 11 July 1657 in Konigsberg. Died 25 February 1713 in Berlin. During his reign, Brandenburg, due to its loyalty to the Holy Roman Emperor, was granted the right to become a kingdom in 1700. Brandenburg therefore became the Kingdom of Prussia with Elector Frederick III becoming Frederick I of Prussia. A patron of the arts and sciences, he founded both the *Akademie der Künste* (Prussian Academy of Art) and *the Akademie der Wissenschaften* (Prussian Academy of Science).

Frederick Wilhelm I of Prussia (1713 - 1740)
Born in Berlin 14 August 1688. Died 31 May 1740 in Berlin. He built a powerful standing army of 89,000, which he forced upon his reluctant son. He created the canton system whereby regiments were able to conscript those peasants who were considered expendable to the local economy. He is credited with co-opting the *Junkers* into royal service by filling the officer corps with their sons. He loved the military and was dubbed *le Roi Sergeant* by George I of England to whom he was related through his mother.

Frederick II of Prussia (1740 - 1786)
Born 24 January 1712 in Berlin. Died 17 August 1786 in Potsdam. Although not really interested in military affairs as a young man, he did well once he inherited the throne and set his mind to making Prussia a European power. Certainly, the most famous of his family line, he came to be better known to us as *Frederick the Great* or more affectionately to the Germans as *der alte Fritz* (Old Fritz). He is recognized as the father of both Germany and the German military. He fought three Silesian wars, the third most known as the Seven Years' War. His genius was not just geo-political; he was a brilliant, if utterly ruthless battlefield commander. At the Battle of Kolin, where he would suffer defeat at the hands of the Austrians, he reputedly screamed at his Guards Regiment (who were hesitating) *Kerls, wollt ihr ewig lebe?* (Scoundrels, would you live forever?)

Frederick Wilhelm II of Prussia (1786 - 1797)
Born 25 September 1744 in Berlin. Died 16 November 1794 in Potsdam. The weak and profligate nephew of *Frederick the Great* was unable to maintain intact the powerful machinery of state, which he

inherited from his famous uncle. During his reign, both the army and the state began a slow and steady decline, which would lead to near ruin.

Frederick Wilhelm III of Prussia (1797 - 1840)
Born 3 August 1770 in Potsdam. Died 7 June 1840 in Berlin. Like his father, this weak son of *Frederick Wilhelm II* led Prussia into disaster during the Napoleonic Wars. Luckily, his army and the country were pulled out of their decline by generals Gerhard David von Scharnhorst and August Neithardt von Gneisenau. To be fair to him, it was not for lack of trying that he was so unsuccessful. Neither he, nor his father, had inherited their ancestor's genius for ruling (or fighting).

Frederick Wilhelm IV of Prussia (1840 – 1861)
Born 15 October 1795 in Berlin. Died 2 January 1861 in Potsdam. Due to illness, he abdicated in favour of his brother in 1857.

Wilhelm I of Prussia (1857 - 1888)
Born 22 March 1797 in Berlin. Died 9 March 1888 in Berlin. Wilhelm ruled initially as Prince Regent (1857 – 1861) and was the last king of Prussia. In 1871, he became the first Emperor of a united Germany as *Kaiser* Wilhelm I Germany.

Frederick III (1888)
Born 18 October 1831 in Potsdam. Died 15 June 1888 in Potsdam. Known as the unfortunate Kaiser, he ruled for a mere ninety-nine days. He is little known since his son Wilhelm II eclipsed him.

Wilhelm II of Germany (1888 - 1918)
Born 27 January 1859 in Berlin. Died 4 June 1941 in Doorn, Netherlands. Grandson of Queen Victoria, he was the last of his line to sit as a reigning monarch. He is surpassed in his fame only by his ancestor *Frederick the Great*. Wilhelm is infamous for militarism, his desire to give the German *Reich* 'a place in the sun' and his alleged precipitation of the First World War in 1914. He abdicated in favour of a republic in 1918, on the advice of the Chief of the Great General Staff, General Eric Ludendorff and died in exile in the Netherlands in June 1941.

Feldmarshal, August Neidhardt Graf von Gneisenau
Lithograph Artist Unknown

ANNEX B: CHIEFS OF THE GENERAL STAFF

Note: The ranks, structures and titles of the men who headed the various incarnations of the General Staff have been intentionally simplified.

Generalleutnant Levin von Geusau (1803 - 1807).
Born 15 October 1734 in Creuzburg, Thuringia, he joined a Prussian fusilier regiment in October 1752 as a ranker. After his appointment as *Portepeefähnrich* and commissioning, King Friedrich Wilhelm II appointed him as his adjutant. In 1790 he was promoted to *Generalmajor* and made head of the *Feldjägerkorps*. He was afterwards made *Generalquartiermeister*. In 1803 his title was changed due to a military reorganization. As a result of this restructure, he also directed the War Department. He was a Grand Master of the Masons and in 1805 he was knighted in the Order of the Black Eagle, Prussia's highest military order. He died in Berlin 27 December 1808.

General David Graf Gerhard von Scharnhorst (1807 - 1813).
Born near Hanover on 12 November 1755 and was commissioned in 1788 into the Hanoverian army as an artillery officer. A highly competent and intellectual officer he published manuals as well as studies of military theory. In 1796 he was promoted to major and stayed until 1801 when he was offered a lieutenant-colonel's commission in the Prussian army. Upon transferring, the king made him a *Graf*, thereby adding 'von' to his name. He was an instructor at

the *Kriegsakademie* as well as tutor to the Prussian crown prince. He commanded a brigade in 1804-5 during which time he was also the Prussian *Quartiermeister*. In 1806, as the Chief of Staff to the Duke of Brunswick he was wounded at the Battle of Auerstädt and captured with Blücher. He became the *de facto* Chief of the General Staff from 1807, when he reorganized the Prussian army because of the defeat at Jena. He selected and appointed his previous students, Wilhelm von Grolman, Carl von Clausewitz, August von Gneisenau, and Hermann von Boyen to key posts. He was wounded at Lützen 2 May 1813 and died of his wounds six weeks later in Prague on 28 June 1813.

Generalfeldmarschall
August Anton Graf Neidhardt von Gneisenau (1813 - 1815).
Born 27 October 1760 in Schildau, Saxony, he served briefly in the Austrian cavalry (1778-80) before heading to Canada as a mercenary in the Ansbach Regiment as a *Leutnant* (1782-83). Commissioned into the Prussian army as a *Hauptman* in 1786, he spent the next 20 years forgotten on garrison duty. The Napoleonic Wars brought him to the attention of the king. Gneisenau fought at Jena in 1806 and distinguished himself as a field commander in the defense of Colberg. He worked with Scharnhorst from 1807-1813 as a reformer, in the establishment of a formal General Staff and the creation of the *Krümper* system for rebuilding the Prussian army by using reserve and territorial forces. He was Blücher's chief of staff in 1813, after Scharnhorst's death. In 1815 he returned for the Waterloo campaign. When Blücher was wounded, he famously decided to withdraw the corps to Wavre, an act that save the Prussians and made possible their support for Wellington. Shortly after the war, he fell out with the king and was removed.

He served briefly as governor of Berlin and then was promoted to *Generalfeldmarschall* in 1825 when he was given command of the Observation Army which was sent to protect Prussia's border during the Polish insurrection of 1831. As Scharnhorst's friend and successor his attempts to promote liberal reforms in the army were thwarted by the reactionary Prussian *Junker* aristocracy. Like Clausewitz, he died of cholera, but much later at the age of 71. He died in Posen 23 August 1831.

General Karl Wilhelm Georg von Grolman (1815 - 1819).
Born in Berlin 30 July 1777. He joined the infantry at age 14. In the rank of *Hauptman*, he was initially an adjutant and then served on the General Staff of an army corps. He was wounded at the Battle of Soldau in 1806 and received the *Pour le Mérite*. Scharnhorst appointed him to the Commission for the Reorganization of the Army in 1807. When Austria declared war on Napoleon, he left the Prussian army to fight with them. After the armistice of 1810, he defied Scharnhorst and went to Spain as a battalion commander of the Spanish Foreign Legion (*Tercio Extranjero*), and in January 1812 became a French prisoner. In the spring of 1813 Grolman re-joined the Prussian army as a general staff officer and was quickly promoted to *Generalmajor* in May 1814 where he served in Blücher's headquarters. Grolman was made Chief of Staff after the departure of Gneisenau after Waterloo. In 1816, he split the staff into three sections, each with responsibility for a potential theatre of war, and added the Military History Section. In 1819, Boyen, who was Minister of War, resigned over the issue of the employment of the *Landwehr* (the Prussian Militia), and Grolman followed him into retirement. He later returned to the army as commander of the 9th Division in Glogau in 1825. From 1833 until his death, he was Commanding General of V Army Corps in Posen. He died on 15 September 1843.

Generalleutnant Rühle von Lilienstern (1819 - 1821).
He was born 16 April 1780, in Berlin. In 1793 he joined the cadet corps in Berlin and at the end of 1795 he joined the elite Garde Regiment in Potsdam as a *Fahnenjunker*. From 1801 he was a member of Scharnhorst's *Militärische Gesellschaft*. As well as being a soldier, he was a polymath, intellectual, and prolific writer. He studied at Scharnhorst's Academy for Officers in the same promotion as Clausewitz. Later, they both taught at the Prussian *Kriegsakademie*, and Rühle became Clausewitz's eventual successor as director. Many of their common views can be traced to their tutelage by Scharnhorst. In 1804 he joined the recently created General Staff and fought at both Jena and Auerstädt. After the defeat, he took leave and moved to Dresden to write. In 1807, he published a book about his work on Hohenlohe-Ingelfingen's staff during the Jena battle and consequently

was taken on as tutor to Prince Bernhard of Weimar, fighting against Austria with a commission in the Saxon army. Early in 1813 he returned to Prussian service and was appointed to von Blücher's headquarters. He took part in the Battle of Leipzig. Late that year, he was promoted to *Oberstleutnant* and put in charge of Prussian re-armament. Soon after Napoleon's return he was promoted to *Oberst*. After Waterloo he returned to Berlin, where he continued to work in various official positions on the Great General Staff. He was made interim Chief after Grolman's departure. In January 1820 he was promoted *Generalmajor* but in 1821, had to relinquish that post to von Müffling due to the latter's seniority. In 1835 he was promoted to *Generalleutnant.* He died in Salzburg on 1 July 1847.

Generalfeldmarschall Karl *Freiherr* von Müffling *(1821 - 1829)*

He was born in Halle, Prussia, on 12 June 1775. In 1787 he joined a fusilier battalion, with which he went to Silesia in 1790 and took part in the campaign against France in 1792/94. From 1797 to 1802 he was employed in the trigonometric measurement of Westphalia, then in 1803 as a *Leutnant* in Thuringia. In 1804, he was admitted to the General Staff and shortly thereafter joined Scharnhorst's *Militärische Gesellschaft.* In 1805 he joined Blücher's staff and took part in the ill-fated battles at Jena and Auerstädt. After his release from captivity, like Lilienstern, he took a commission in the Saxon army. In April 1813 he returned to Prussian service and was admitted to the General Staff as an *Oberstleutnant*, and in June he was again assigned to Blücher. Despite the objections of Gneisenau, Müffling became a *Quartiermeister* of the Army of Silesia in the rank of *Oberst*. In December 1813 he was appointed a *Generalmajor*, and after seizing Paris in June 1814 was awarded the *Pour le Mérite* with oak leaves.

Napoleon's escape from Elba saw Müffling sent to the Duke of Wellington's headquarters as a liaison officer. After Waterloo, he was military governor of Paris for several months. In the spring of 1816, he returned to the General Staff to work in the topographical section, eventually heading it and in April 1818 he was promoted to *Generalleutnant.* In 1819, he refused the position of Prussian envoy in London, preferring to work on the topography of the Rhine. On the 11th of January 1821 he became Chief of the General Staff, a position he held for eight years. He left in November 1829 to serve as commander of the VII Army Corps. In March 1838 he became the Governor of Berlin. He retired from active service on the 5th of October 1847 with a promotion to *Generalfeldmarschall* and died in Erfurt 10 January 1851.

General Wilhelm von Krauseneck *(1829 - 1848)*

He was born in Bayreuth, Bavaria, on 13 October 1774. In 1791, he became a cadet in the Ansbach artillery. He was also interested in topography and military engineering. He participated in the 1793-94 campaign in France. In 1807 he fought at Heilsberg and Eylau, winning the *Pour le Mérite*. In 1813, at Lützen, like Scharnhorst he was wounded in action while on Blücher's staff. Krauseneck thereafter served as commandant of the fortresses in Graudenz and Mainz. He culminated his distinguished military career by serving for twenty years as Prussian Chief of General Staff from 1829-49. In 1849 he resigned to become a royal envoy. Krauseneck was a liberal and spent much of his tenure fighting the rise of Prussian militarism. He died 2 November 1850 in Berlin.

Generalleutnant Karl von Reyher *(1849 - 1857)*

He was born on 21 June 1786, in Groß Schönebeck, Prussia the son of a professor. In 1802 he joined the army as an infantry company clerk. He joined the *Freikorps* after Jena working his way to sergeant major. In 1810 he was commissioned in the Prussian army and fought throughout the Napoleonic Wars, after which he served with the occupation forces in France. He continued to serve including on the General staff and was ennobled in 1818.

He served briefly (several weeks) as Minister of War in 1848, and the following year became Chief of the General Staff. He was a strong believer in the strategic importance of railway networks and spent a great deal of his tenure working to defend the unique position of the General Staff against those who would see it diminished. He died in Berlin on 7 October 1857.

Generalfeldmarschall Helmuth Carl Bernhard *Graf* von Moltke *(1857 - 1888)*

He was born 26 October 1800 in Parchim, Mecklenburg-Vorpommern. Moltke is arguably the most famous officer ever to hold the office of Chief of the Great General Staff. He made significant technical, tactical, and structural changes to the General Staff, elevating it to its greatest height, in terms of power and influence. His philosophical changes would last well into the following century and continue to have some relevance up to the present day. From 1882, he had *Graf* von Waldersee as his deputy. In 1888, he was finally allowed to resign his post in favour of his deputy. He died 24 April 1891 in Berlin.

Generalfeldmarschall
Alfred Ludwig Heinrich Karl *Graf* von Waldersee *(1888-1891)*
He was born 8 April 1832 in Potsdam, Prussia. Moltke groomed Waldersee to replace him. Openly anti-Semitic and a religious zealot, he was not on good terms with some members of the royal family nor the chancellor Otto *Prinz* von Bismarck. Wilhelm II and Waldersee did not see eye to eye and after an incident during the 1890 army manoeuvres, the Kaiser had his Chief of Staff moved out of office and replaced by *Generalfeldmarschall* Alfred *Graf* von Schlieffen, who remained in office until 1906. He died on 5 March 1904 in Hanover.

Generalfeldmarschall Alfred *Graf* von Schlieffen *(1891-1906)*
He was born in Berlin 28 February 1833, son of a Prussian army officer. Academically inclined, he trained for a career in law but was commissioned into the 2nd Guards Uhlans Regiment in 1853. He attended the *Kriegsakademie* 1858-61 and joined the General Staff in 1865. Saw action in both the Austro-Prussian and the Franco-Prussian wars, after which he commanded the 1st Guards Uhlans Regiment. Became deputy to Waldersee in 1888 and succeeded him in 1891. He was convinced that Germany would have to fight outnumbered and believed the key to victory could be discovered by studying the Battle of Cannae. He ordered the General Staff Historical Section to create Cannae Studies (still used by the *Führungsakademie* to this day and deeply ingrained in German tactical thinking) that would demonstrate the principle of double envelopment and eventually created his plan to beat Russia and France in succession. He died 4 January 1913 in Berlin, having continued to refine his plan after retirement.

General Helmuth Johannes Ludwig *Graf* von Moltke *(1906-1916)*
Born 25 May 1848 in Gersdorff, Mecklenburg. Joined the Prussian army in 1870 but did not see action. Nephew and adjutant to his more famous uncle Helmuth. Commanded a Guards Corps division and became deputy to Schlieffen in 1904. Without a strong enough personality to confront the belligerent and adventuristic Kaiser. His legacy was his weakening of his predecessor's eponymous invasion plan. Died 18 June 1916 in Potsdam.

General Erich von Falkenhayn *(1914-1916)*
Born 11 November 1861 in Burg Belchau, Prussia to an old *Junker* family. Joined the army as a cadet in the infantry. Was a military instructor and saw action in China during the Boxer Rebellion (1900-01). Was Minister of War in 1913 and retained that post when appointed by *Kaiser* Wilhelm II to replace Moltke after the defeat at the Marne in September 1914. Relieved by the Kaiser after Verdun in December 1916. He died 8 April 1922 in Potsdam.

Generalfeldmarschall
Paul Ludwig Hans von Hindenburg *(1916-1918)*
He was born on 2 October 1847 in Poznan, Poland, son of a Prussian army officer. Joined the Royal Cadet Corps in 1860 and was commissioned into the Foot Guards in 1866. He saw action in many battles. Attended the *Kriegsakademie* 1872-1875 and joined the General Staff shortly thereafter. Won a stunning victory as the commander against the Russians at Tannenberg in 1914. Appointed by the Kaiser to replace Falkenhayn, and because of Wilhelm's weakness, he soon became *de facto* military dictator of Germany, removing the chancellor, Theobald von Bethmann-Hollweg, in 1917. Was elected President of the Weimar Republic in 1925 and appointed Adolf Hitler as chancellor on the advice of Franz von Papen in 1933. He died on 2 August 1934 at his estate near Neudeck in East Prussia (now Poland).

Prince Frederick Charles of Prussia
Image from journal Die Gartenlaube, 1885.

ANNEX C: MISSION ANALYSIS

His Majesty made you a major because he believed you would know when not to obey his orders.

- Prinz Frederick Charles

ission analysis (*Auswertung des Auftrages*) is the soul of *Auftragstaktik*. To attempt to employ *Auftragstaktik* without fully understanding Mission analysis is simply not possible. A mission analysis is a detailed examination of the tasks that a military commander has been given from a higher commander; it is a *mission evaluation*. It is an essential tool for leaders and their subordinates to ensure that there is unity of purpose throughout their organizations and, contrary to what some believe, a mission analysis is an ongoing process; it never stops. Like a virus checker that constantly runs on a personal computer, it may not always be apparent but is constantly ongoing.

The purpose of this procedure is not only to produce a mission, but also and just as importantly, to allow the subordinate commander to fully appreciate the tasks and the purposes behind those tasks. Mission analysis compels a commander to understand and work within her superior's intent. A corner stone of German tactical doctrine is the belief that all commanders act independently and with resolute action. Leaders are not to wait for direction; they are to exploit a situation on their own initiative based on what they derived from their mission analysis. All commanders within the chain of command have a shared responsibility to achieve their superior commander's intent. As Dr MacAndrew said, this concept makes soldiers *shareholders of operations, rather than un-consulted employees.* This tool applies a conceptual brake on commanders who may attempt to act in isolation or to change the overall aim. In other words, subordinate commanders who act completely outside the scope of the commander's aim are acting irresponsibly and will be treated accordingly. Thus, a measure of self-reliance and initiative is passed to the subordinate commander who is often in a much better position than his superior to make responsible, timely decisions which will aid in the success of the plan.

So, you have received your orders and now it is time to complete your mission analysis. We need to deconstruct the process to see what it means to you as a commander:

The first step is always to identify the enemy's and the superior commanders' intent (at least two levels up). In this way, knowing what the enemy intends and your commander's intent, as well as the next senior commander's intent, allows you to contextualize what your superiors want to achieve and how you fit into those intentions. In this way, you can shape your own intent so that it dovetails with theirs. This consideration helps you to understand what your role is in their overall plan.

The next step is to review all that you have been asked to do. What are the tasks, both stated and implied? It is critical that you tease out not just those obvious tasks that have been assigned to you, but also those tasks that are implied or have not been plainly stated. You must fully understand everything that needs to be accomplished by you and your forces. That understanding leads you to determine the one task upon which everything depends; this task becomes your mission. If you have been given a mission like **1st Troop will seize Objective A** this statement *may* survive the mission analysis to become your mission, but until you have gone through the process it is just one of your tasks.

Once all the tasks have been identified, you need to determine all limitations upon your freedom of action, however they have been stated. These limitations are considered as two distinct types: constraints (must do) and restraints (must not do). This consideration stems from the Prussian army reforms instituted by Field Marshall Helmuth von Moltke the Elder in the late 1860s. Moltke insisted that all commanders needed to have freedom of action (*Freiheit des Handelns*) while working within their superior commanders' intent. Thus, the two questions: what *must* I do and what must I *not* do?

By now your brain will have precipitated a mission. Having looked at all the data, one of the tasks is certain to jump out at you as your obvious mission. But you are not finished yet. You have one final step before declaring what your mission is. This final step of mission analysis, and the one least understood, is arguably the most critical. Ask yourself: Considering the current situation, is my current mission *still* valid? In other words, has the situation changed fundamentally? If this is your initial mission analysis, then the answer is highly likely **yes** and your mission is clear. Remember my comment about this being an ongoing process? Here we have the so-called virus checker that constantly runs through the commander's subconscious. All leaders must constantly review the current situation to determine if there has been a fundamental change which would re-initiate a mission analysis. In this final step, you determine (consciously or subconsciously) if your commander would still assign these tasks in this changed situation. In other words: If the answer is **yes**, then keep going. If the answer is **no**, then you need to restart a mission analysis to determine what the mission now is. Thus, mission analysis never ends.

Enough of hypotheticals, time to consider an elementary example. You are a reconnaissance troop commander who has been called on the secure radio by your squadron commander.

She says "Jessie, higher needs to immediately take control of several choke points that intersect route AJAX. One of them is a road junction on route AJAX approximately one kilometer north of your current location. There are no known enemy between you and the junction. I need you to prove route AJAX and visually clear it of enemy to 100 metres either side of AJAX. I also need you to clear the building at the road junction. The junction must be under your control before last light today, but you must not depart your current location before 1300 hours since there is activity near that junction that you cannot be a part of. Use the few hours between now and then to give your troops some rest. You will establish an all-round hasty defence of the junction no later than 0100 hours tomorrow. The sergeant-major will resupply you at first light plus 30 minutes tomorrow. He will approach from the west on route ARGO so you will need a contact point on that route to meet him and guide him into your position. Acknowledge."

You acknowledge her orders and immediately begin your battle procedure. Your mission analysis:

The brigade needs to control all the choke points that cut across AJAX. By looking at the map you see only one in this sector, so your squadron got tasked and your squadron commander has given it to you. Obviously, she thinks that you can do this with your troop, or she would have taken the task herself. Just the same, it is important to her, and you must succeed, or she will need to come and fix it. You are clear on your squadron commander's intent. What about the battle group commander? He wants to control the choke points across AJAX. Clear enough.

You ask yourself: What do I need to accomplish?

1. Visually clear the route AJAX 100 hundred metres either side (assigned).
2. Prove route AJAX from here to the road junction (assigned).
3. Control the junction (assigned).
4. Clear the building at the junction (assigned).
5. Establish an all-round hasty defence at the junction (assigned).

6. Establish a contact point on route ARGO to the west of junction (assigned).

At this point your mind momentarily wanders off and you ask yourself why you joined the cavalry and not the air force like your older brother.... The troop warrant officer interrupts your thoughts.

"You OK, sir?"

"Yes warrant, thanks. The major just called with new orders. Drop the sentries to one per patrol, put everyone on forced rest for the next two hours. Tell the patrol commanders that we are now on 15 minutes notice to move. Then please come back and I will brief you. Oh yes, one more thing, have the troop sergeant do a quick inventory of our defensive stores. Thanks, warrant." As he walks away you return to your tasks.

1. Put everyone on forced rest (implied).
2. Change the notice to move (implied).
3. Do an inventory of defence stores (implied)

You think you got them all, but you are confident that your warrant officer and sergeant will make sure nothing is missed. Among all these tasks, one is key to the whole operation. This will become your mission. You think for a few seconds. **Defend**. The all-round defence is the key to accomplishing what the squadron commander and the battle group commander need accomplished. This becomes your mission, and you say it aloud to yourself: **1st Troop will defend road junction at grid 798 574.**

Time to look at limitations. You CANNOT depart this location before 1300 hours. You MUST put at least one vehicle physically on the road all the way to the junction (prove the route). You MUST be defensible by no later than 0100 hours tomorrow. OK, none of these limitations impinges upon your ability to achieve the mission.

Last step. Has the situation changed fundamentally? Yes, I was in a waiting posture and am now pursuing a new mission. My mission of "defend" is valid, but I will have to keep an open mind should I encounter unforeseen enemy on my way to the objective.

As you start to compose your verbal orders the troop warrant sits down next to you. He hands you a cup of fresh coffee. "OK, sir. All the troops getting ready for a new mission. What's up?"

✠ ✠ ✠

We have looked at an elementary situation where the tasks were both simple and straightforward. That is not to say that troop leader Jessie will not run into trouble. Moltke's famous dictum that no plan ever survives first contact with the enemy, means that battles rarely unfold as foreseen. Every commander must be constantly vigilant for changing situations. Situational awareness is therefore paramount even above freedom of action. Only if a commander fully understands his superiors' intent can he hope to act within the boundaries of that intent when the situation does change. In this case we are beginning with a fresh start, but the situation may change as soon as the troops head out onto the route and a commander must be aware of both the current situation and what is expected of him. Further, he needs his own troops to be in the same frame of mind. When subordinates understand the intent and everyone is confident that they can act freely to alter the mission to remain within the intent, the mission analysis has been effective and the concept of *Auftragstaktik* is at work.

Nota Bene: This fundamentally German process has been modified by most NATO countries. The original German process, though similar, is not identical. Canada, Britain, France, and the US have all created their own versions. In fact, within the US military, the version of mission analysis changes with each of the branches. Below is the German process:

Superiors' Intent
What is the critical task expected of me?
What are the restrictions to my freedom of action?
Has the situation changed fundamentally?
What must be done now?

Kaiser Wilhelm II
Photo by T.H. Voigt, 1904

ANNEX D: CIVILIAN LEADERSHIP

When one treats people with benevolence, justice and righteousness, and reposes confidence in them, the army will be united in mind and will be happy to serve their leaders.

- Sun Tzu

An appropriate way to end this investigation into the birth of enlightened leadership is to recall that leadership is not purely the domain of military forces. Society has a great need for leadership of all types and forms. From being a chief executive officer of a corporation to managing a grocery store to being a parent, leadership skills are inevitably in great demand and in too scarce supply. But I must warn that in the same way that non-German militaries cannot simply 'graft' the concept of *Auftragstaktik* onto their command-and-control systems, civilian leaders and managers cannot simply grab a book from the shelf describing tools and techniques of *Auftragstaktik* and expect successful outcomes overnight. Further, beware of the genius of marketing gurus expounding on how simple it is to adopt 'transformational leadership' or 'follower leadership' or 'flat organizational leadership'.

It is practically impossible to pass an entire day without seeing, hearing, or using words, ideas, or concepts related to war. Western society appears convinced that it is in some way or other continually at war with something. Consumers are inundated daily with the analogies, metaphors, and images of war. North America is in the middle of a *war* on poverty. The Western world has been losing a *war* against drugs for decades. There is an ongoing *war* against illiteracy. Fox News annually claims that there is a *war* against Christmas. America has declared a *war* against terrorism. As further proof of the widespread misuse of bellicose words and concepts, consider the many professional groups that have adopted military vocabularies. Stockbrokers *fight* desperate actions in the financial *trenches* to *secure the perimeter* of corporate profits. Medical doctors launch *counterattacks* against AIDS and cancer. Dentists *bombard* their patients with x-rays. Barristers *gird their loins for combat in the arena* of jurisprudence.

Naturally, most of this misuse is merely literary license. During the so-called cola wars Coke and Pepsi never actually fought each other. It can be exciting for people to use the aphorisms and metaphors of heroic struggles. To most of the populace this language somehow makes the mundane seem important. In a world of bellicose adages, the drudgery of making money takes on the importance of a Homeric quest. Selling the latest computer software becomes as urgent as winning a pitched battle. Such language lends an air of authority to ordinary tasks, irrespective of their actual importance. There is also a sense of clarity when at war; the enemy is defined, and the nation united in a struggle against a common foe. Calling something a war does not make it so.

The point of this hyperbole is that the world of business and commerce is besotted with military imagery and with many leadership concepts taken from the military. To be fair, if the leadership philosophy that the military uses can convince people to lay down their lives for a mission, it is not unreasonable to believe that there may be something of value in that leadership to help corporations and organizations become better at what they do and thereby also become more profitable and more effective. Many obviously think so and I would agree. Consider the number of books available with titles like *Sun Tzu and the Art of Business* or the essay "Fighting Your Business Battles: 6 Lasting Lessons From Sun Tzu's *Art of War,*" or some such conflation of war and commerce, which explain how you can use this ancient text to maximize your leadership and your profits. These texts far outnumber the translated versions of Sun Tzu's original *Art of War*. It may seem odd to soldiers or military historians, but these people have a good point. Successful military leadership, which has been developed and fine-tuned over generations does have something to offer the non-military leaders in society, whether they are in the corporate world, the medical professions, teaching, or even charitable organizations. In short, *Auftragstaktik* can be a useful philosophy for any type of leader anywhere and at any time. A short example helps illustrate the point: Years ago, in my last position in the Regular Army, I was the Chief of Staff of the Canadian Army Command and Staff College. About half of the people that worked for me were civilian employees, some clerical, some maintenance. The other half were uniformed personnel of all ranks. On the first day after I took over, I gathered all the college staff in the main lecture theatre. From gardeners to cleaning staff, from military training staff to secretaries and librarians, I gave them a ten-minute basic lecture on *Auftragstaktik* and then I said:

> I hereby empower each one of you to decide on the spot if a decision is required. If your decision turns out to have been wrong, you will not be punished or chastised. However, if you saw that a decision was needed and did not decide to make the situation better, I will be disappointed.

There was a silence, then one of the secretaries asked how that affected her. I said that perhaps she might be working late on a training course package and someone from the printing office might call needing urgent permission to print extra copies of the course joining instructions. Those instructions were the purview of the military operations staff, but they had left for a long weekend. You could simply tell the printing office to wait until after the holiday when the Operations Major came back but better still, knowing that the need was both legitimate and urgent, you could give the printing office permission and then put a note on the Operations Major's desk explaining your decision.

She beamed. "Really?" she asked.

"Really." I replied.

For the next few weeks as I made my daily walk around the college talking to the staff, I was constantly engaged by subordinates who were thrilled to have been empowered as never before. It was infrequent that any of them had to take decisions as I had laid out but occasionally it happened, and I always made a point of publicly praising those individuals at my weekly conference. A couple of times poor choices were made but again, I praised them for their initiative. It did not take long for the staff to understand that they really did have the power to make the college work better and they joyfully embraced that power. To borrow Professor McAndrew's words, again, I had made them *shareholders of operations* and not just *un-consulted employees*.

Thus, *Auftragstaktik* need not be restricted to purely military or tactical applications. There is no reason that this leadership philosophy will not work in a non-military setting. After all, empowering subordinates is a universal leadership and management tool. As I implied, bookstore shelves are filled with tomes describing 'Servant' leadership or 'Transformational' leadership or 'Follower' leadership. This is old wine in new bottles.

Whatever your trade or profession, your subordinates are capable, intelligent, and most importantly, have great amounts of initiative. You need to recognize and reward these characteristics and traits. Further, you need to seek more responsibility from your superiors and demonstrate your commitment to the success of their mission. Then you need to do the same with your subordinates. You need to demonstrate daily that you are willing to accept more independence from your subordinates, that organizational missions are *shared* responsibilities and that you expect them to carry out the mission despite a breakdown in communications or the removal of any leader in the chain of command. Most important, you need to earn their trust.

BIBLIOGRAPHY

Note on sources. This book is based on the research done for my MA thesis, which spawned from the good fortune of having had many conversations with German war veterans on the subject. These conversations included interviews with Oberst Hans von Luck, Commander of Panzergrenadier-regiment 125 in Normandy, SS Oberstürmbahnführer Hubert Meyer, Chief of General Staff of 12. SS-Panzerdivision 'Hitlerjugend', in Normandy, and Oberst Gerhard Muhm, who, as an Oberleutnant, won an Iron Cross for his leadership of a Panzergrenadiercompanie against Canada's Royal 22nd Regiment in Italy. Much of the body of thought in this book is a result of my two years of study at the FüAk and the subsequent five years of contact with the Bundeswehr. Consequently, in some cases the ideas are the outgrowth of my training as a Generalstabsoffizier. Errors of interpretation are my own.

Books

Abenheim, D. *Reforging the Iron Cross: the search for tradition in the West German Armed Forces*, Princeton, NJ: Princeton University Press, 1988.

Berghahn, Volker. *Militarism: The History of an International Debate, 1861 - 1979*, (Leamington Spa, UK: Berg Publishing, 1981).

Carr, William. *The Origins of the German Wars of Unification*, New York: Longman, 1991).

Citino, Robert M. *The Quest for Decisive Victory: From Stalemate to Blitzkrieg in Europe, 1899-1940*, Lawrence, KS: University of Kansas Press, 2002.

Clemente, Steven. *For King and Kaiser! The Making of the Prussian Army Officer, 1860-1914*, Westport CT: Greenwood Press, 1992.

von Cochenhausen, Friedrich. *Von Scharnhorst zu Schliefen 1806-1906: Hundert Jahre Preußisch-Deutscher Generalstab, auf Verlassung des Reichwehrministeriums*, Berlin: E.S. Mittler, 1933.

Cooper, Matthew. *The German Army 1933-1945: Its Political and Military Failure*, New York: Bonanza Books, 1984.

Carstem, F. L. *Essays in German History*, London: Hambledon Press, 1985.

Cessford, Michael P. "Warriors for the Working Day", Unpublished PhD dissertation: Carleton University, 1996.

Craig, Gordon, A. *The Politics of the Prussian Army 1640-1945*, Oxford: Oxford University Press, 1955.

van Creveld, Martin. *Command in War*, London: Harvard University Press, 1985.

_____ *Fighting Power: German and U.S. Army Fighting Performance, 1939 – 1945*, Westport CT: Praeger, 1982.

Demeter, Karl. *The German Officer-Corps in Society and State 1650-1945*, Angus Malcolm trans., London: Weidenfeld and Nicolson, 1965.

DePuy William, *Generals Balck and von Mellenthin on Tactics: Implications for Military Doctrine*, BDM Corporation, December 1980, reproduced and edited by Reiner K. Huber, München: Universität der Bundeswehr, 2004.

Dupuy, T.N. *A Genius for War: The German Army and General Staff, 1807 – 1945*, (Englewood Cliffs, NJ: Prentice-Hall, 1977).

Demeter, Karl. *The German Officer-Corps in Society and State 1650 -1945*. Angus Malcolm trans., London: Weidenfeld and Nicolson, 1965.

Fischer, Fritz. *From Kaiserreich to Third Reich, Elements of Continuity in German History, 1871 - 1945*, Roger Fletcher trans., Winchester, MA: Allen & Unwin, 1986

Friederich, R. *Erzieher des Preußischen Heeres Band 6 – Gneisenau,*

Berlin, 1906.

Frederick the Great. *Instructions for his Generals*, in *Roots of Strategy*, Thomas R. Phillips, ed., Harrisburg, PA: Stackpole Books, 1985.

Görlitz, Walter. *History of the German General Staff 1657-1945*. Brian Battershaw trans., New York: Praeger, 1961.

Grunberger, Richard. *The 12-Year Reich: A Social History of Nazi Germany 1933-1945*, New York: Ballentine Books, 1971.

Holborn, Hajo "The Prusso-German School: Moltke and the Rise of the General Staff" in *Makers of Modern Strategy: from Machiavelli to The Nuclear Age*, Peter Paret, ed., Princeton, NJ: Princeton University Press, 1986.

Howard, Michael. *The Franco-Prussian War, The Franco-Prussian War: The German Invasion of France, 1870-1871*, London: Routledge, 1962.

_____ *War in European History*, London: Oxford University Press, 1976.

Jones, Archer. *The Art of War in the Western World*, New York: Oxford University Press, 1989.

Kitchen, Martin. *A Military History of Germany from the Eighteenth Century to the Present Day*, London: Weidenfeld and Nicholson, 1975.

von Lignitz, Viktor. *Erzieher des Preußischen Heeres Band 5 – Scharnhorst*, Berlin:B. Behr's Verlag, 1905.

Lind, William S. *Maneuver Warfare Handbook*, Boulder CO, Routledge, 1985.

Maier, Charles S. *The Unmasterable Past: History, Holocaust and German National Identity*, Cambridge, MA: Harvard University Press, 1988.

MacGregor, Douglas A. *Breaking the Phalanx A New Design for Landpower in the 21st Century*, Westport CT: Praeger, 1997.

McElwee, William. *The Art of War Waterloo to Mons,* Bloomington, IN: Indiana University Press, 1974.

Messenger, Charles. *The Blitzkrieg Story*, New York: Scribner, 1976.

Millotat, Christian. *Understanding the Prussian-German General Staff System*, (Carlisle Barracks, PA: US Army War College,

1992.

Muhm, Gerhard. "La tattica tedesca nella campagna d'Italia" in *linea Gotica: avamposto dei Balcani,* Amadeo Montemaggi, ed., Roma, 1993.

Oetting, Dirk W. *Auftragstaktik: Geschichte und Gegenwart einer Führungskonzeption*, Frankfurt am Main: Report Verlag, 1993.

Ohis, Gary J. *The Operational Leadership of Helmuth von Moltke*, (Monograph, US Naval War College, 1994.

Oppenheim, Walter. *Habsburgs* and *Hohenzollerns 1713-1786*, London: Hodder & Stoughten, 1993.

Otto, Helmut. *Schlieffen und der Generalstab,* Berlin: Dietz Verlag, 1966.

Palmer, R. R. *The World of the French Revolution*, New York: Harper, 1971.

Parker, Geoffrey. *The Military Revolution, Military Innovation and the Rise of the West*, 1500-1800, Cambridge: Cambridge University Press, 1988.

Planze, Otto. *Bismarck and the Development of Germany*, Vol I: 1815-1879 and Vol II: 1871-1880, Princeton NJ: Princeton University Press, 1990).

Ritter, Gerhard. *The German Problem: Basic Questions of German Political Life, Past and Present*, Columbus Ohio: Ohio State University Press, 1965.

Posen, Barry. *The Sources of Military Doctrine*, Ithaca, NY: Cornell University Press, 1984.

Rosinsky, Herbert. *The German Army*, London: Pall Mall Press, 1966.

Rothenberg, Gunther E. "Moltke, Schlieffen, and the Doctrine of Strategic Envelopment" in *Makers of Modern Strategy: from Machiavelli to The Nuclear Age*, Peter Paret, ed., Princeton NJ: Princeton University Press, 1986.

von Seeckt, Hans. *Thoughts of a Soldier*, Gilbert Waterhouse, trans., London: Ernest Benn, 1930.

Shanahan, Walter O. *Prussian Military Reforms 1786-1813*, New York: Columbia University Press, 1945.

Showalter, Dennis E. "Prussia, Technology and War: Artillery from 1815 to 1914." in *Men, Machines and War: Proceedings of the 11th Military History Symposium,* Royal Military College, Ronald Haycock and Keith Neilson, eds., Waterloo, ON: University of Waterloo Press, 1988.

Summers, Harry, G. Jr. *On Strategy: The Vietnam War in Context,* Carlisle Barracks, PA: U.S. Army War College, 1983.

Wallach, Jehuda L. *The Dogma of the Battle of Annihilation: The Theories of Clausewitz and Schlieffen and Their Impact on the German Conduct of Two World Wars,* Westport, CT: Praeger, 1986.

White, Charles Edward. *The Enlightened Soldier: Scharnhorst and the Militärische Gesellschaft in Berlin, 1801-1805,* Westport, CT: Praeger, 1989.

Westphal, Siegfried. *The German Army in the West,* Toronto: Cassell and Co, 1951.

Wilkinson, Spenser. *The Brain of an Army, A Popular Account of the German General Staff,* London: Macmillan,1890.

Journals and Monographs

Bashista, Ronald J. *"Auftragstaktik:* It's More Than Just a Word" in US Army *Armor,* November-December 1994.

Beaumont, Roger. "Wehrmacht Mystique Revisited" in *Military Review,* February 1990.

Berghahn, Volker. "The Unmastered and Unmasterable Past" a book review of Imanuel Geiß, *Die Habermas - Kontroverse: Ein deutscher Streit,* Charles S. Maier, *The Unmasterable Past: History Holocaust and German National Identity,* and Richard J. Evans, *In Hitler's Shadow: West German Historians and the Attempt to Escape from the Nazi Past,* in *Journal of Modern History,* September 1991.

Brown, John Sloan. "Colonel Trevor N. Dupuy and the Mythos of Wehrmacht Superiority: A Reconsideration", in *Military Affairs,* January 1986.

Carlson, Verner R. "Portrait of a German General Staff Officer" in *Military Review* Leavenworth Kansas, April 1990.

Czeslik, Knut. "Auftragstaktik Thoughts of a German Officer" in

US Army *Infantry*, January-February 1991.

Cowan, David, M. *Auftragstaktik: How low Can You Go?* Monograph at US Army School of Advanced Military Studies, Leavenworth Kansas, December 1986.

van Creveld, Martin. "On Learning from the Wehrmacht and Other Things" in *Military Review*, January 1988.

Echevarria, Antulio J. "Moltke and the German Military Tradition: His Theories and Legacies" in *Parameters*, Spring 1996.

_____ "On the Brink of the Abyss: The Warrior Identity and German Military Thought before the Great War" in *War & Society*, October 1995.

Eisel, George W. *Befehlstaktik and the Red Army Experience: Are There Lessons for Us? Considerations for the Formal Adoption of Auftragstaktik*, Monograph at US Army School of Advanced Military Studies, Leavenworth Kansas, December 1992.

Förster, Stig. "Facing 'People's War': Moltke the Elder and Germany's Military Options after 1871" in *The Journal of Strategic Studies*, June 1987.

Harwood, Michael J. *Auftragstaktik: We Can't Get There From Here*, Monograph at US Army School of Advanced Military Studies, Leavenworth Kansas, June 1990.

Hughes, Daniel J. "Abuses of German Military History" in *Military Review*, December 1986.

Krause, Michael D. "Moltke and the Origins of Operational Art" in *Military Review,* September 1990.

Kerkemeyer, Frank A. "Auftragstaktik" US Army *Infantry*, November-December 1987.

Lorenz, Chris. "Beyond Good and Evil? The German Empire of 1871 and Modern German Historiography" in *The Journal of Contemporary History*, 1995.

Murray, Williamson. "The German Response to Victory in Poland: A Case Study in Professionalism," in *Armed Forces and Society*, Winter 1981.

Nelson, John T. "Where to Go from Here? Considerations for the Formal Adoption of *Auftragstaktik*", Monograph at US Army School of Advanced Military Studies, Leavenworth

Kansas, May 1987.

Poirier, Robert. *General Hans von Seeckt and the Problem of Army Renewal*, RMC War Studies 500 unpublished monograph, Jan 1996.

Silva, John L. "*Auftragstaktik:* Its Origin and Development" in US Army *Infantry*, September-October 1989.

Vermillion, John M. *Tactical Implications of the Adoption of Auftragstaktik for Command and Control on the AirLand Battlefield*, Monograph at US Army School of Advanced Military Studies, Leavenworth Kansas, December 1985.

Walters, Robert G. "Order Out of Chaos: A Case Study of the Application of *Auftragstaktik* by the 11th Panzer Division during the Chir River Battles 7-19 December 1942", Monograph at US Naval Postgraduate School, Monterey CA, 1989.

Generalfeldmarschall **Paul Ludwig Hans von Hindenburg**
Photo by Nicola Perscheid, 1914.

von Hindenburg

INDEX

Reichswehr, 5, 96, 99, 126, 128

PRAXIS
TACTICUM

THE ART, SCIENCE AND
PRACTICE OF MILITARY TACTICS

COLONEL CHARLES S. OLIVIERO

PRAXIS TACTICUM

THE ART, SCIENCE AND PRACTICE OF MILITARY TACTICS

"Praxis Tacticum" will help young leaders learn and master modern combat team tactics...It's a fascinating series of intellectual and practical exercises which will help those leading fast moving and hard-hitting troops in combat, a unique blend of both the science and art of war.

Lieutenant-General (ret'd) The Hon. Andrew Leslie, PC, CMM, MSC, MSM, CD, MA, PhD

Chuck brings the discussion on tactics to the 'centre of gravity' between operational and theoretical perspectives. Praxis Tacticum is for professionals, people interested in tactics and the general reader of history.

Major-General (ret'd) David Fraser, CMM, MSC, MSM, CD

Pundits the world over have long predicted the end of conventional warfare but for the foreseeable future, it is here to stay. Counter insurgency, guerrilla warfare, terrorism, peace enforcement, policing duties. All of these forms, like conventional warfare, are as old as mankind. Modern militaries claim that they are professional bodies, responsible to teach, control and discipline their members. But at least one aspect of this claim is poorly executed: tactics are not taught to junior leaders, which is why this practical guide is essential reading for all junior leaders, officers and NCOs alike.

There is an old military adage that there is no teacher like the enemy. True; but the wise commander will prepare to meet that enemy and become the teacher and not the student.

STRATEGIA

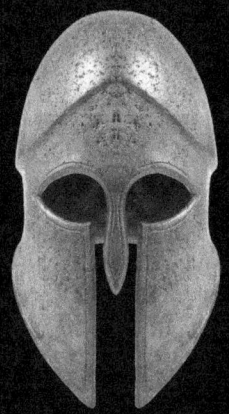

A PRIMER ON THEORY AND STRATEGY
FOR STUDENTS OF WAR

COLONEL CHARLES S. OLIVIERO

STRATEGIA
A PRIMER ON THEORY AND STRATEGY FOR STUDENTS OF WAR

A must read for practitioners and students of the art of war.
LCol Professor David Kilcullen, PHD

These days we fight wars but we do not win them...Colonel Oliviero shows us the way to go at it. The colonel knows the deal.
Daniel P. Bolger, Lieutenant General, US Army, Retired

...a much needed guide to becoming [a] well-informed and deeply versed strategist...free from the curse of parroting bromides they learned at staff college as a substitute for serious and rigorous thought.
Dr. John Grenier, author of The First Way of War

War fascinates us, but what do we really know about its nature?

Strategia is the product of Colonel Oliviero's decades-long intellectual quest to address this fundamental query. His work offers both the serious student and the casual reader a foundation stone upon which to build a deeper understanding of military thought and theory, and thereby a richer appreciation of mankind's deadliest pursuit.

Strategia introduces many of the major contributors to military thought and theory as well as some of their most profound impacts on the conduct of war, from Sun-Tzu to the modern day, encompassing warfare on land, at sea and in the air, as well as in the cyber-realm.

While not an all-encompassing deep dive, Strategia is an essential primer and a point of departure. With this foundation stone in place, the student of war can proceed to follow Clausewitz's admonition to develop a "fine and penetrating mind."

DOUBLE‡DAGGER

— www.doubledagger.ca —

Double Dagger Books is Canada's newest military-focused publisher. Conflict and warfare have shaped human history since before we began to record it. The earliest stories that we know of, passed on as oral tradition, speak of war, and more importantly, the essential elements of the human condition that are revealed under its pressure. We are dedicated to publishing material that, while rooted in conflict, transcends the idea of "war" as merely a genre. Fiction, non- fiction, and stuff that defies categorization, we want to read it all.

Because if you want peace, study war.

ABOUT THE AUTHOR

Colonel (Retired) Chuck Oliviero, CD, PhD is an internationally recognized expert in simulation supported training and has twice been the Keynote Speaker at the international training conferences and fora. He has over four decades' experience as an educator and trainer. For two decades, he was responsible for designing, developing, and delivering some of the most complex collective training events ever conducted in synthetic environments for military, government, and corporate entities. Colonel Oliviero served more than 30 years in the Canadian Forces, retiring as a Colonel. His career included command of Canada's then only tank regiment, the 8th Canadian Hussars (Princess Louise's), establishing Canada's Arms Control Verification Unit and being both an instructor and the Chief of Staff of the Canadian Army Command and Staff College. He is a graduate of the Royal Military College of Canada, holds a BA (Hon) in History, an MA, and a PhD in War Studies. He is also a graduate of the two-year German War College (*Führungsakademie der Bundeswehr*) course. His last military duty was as Special Advisor to the Commander Canadian Army. In 2011 the Minister of National Defence appointed him as Honorary Lieutenant Colonel of the Queen's York Rangers (1st Americans). For more than a decade, he was an Adjunct Professor of history and strategy at both the Royal Military College and Norwich University in Vermont, USA. He is married and has two sons, both of whom are serving officers in the Canadian Armed Forces and Afghanistan veterans.